Haitian Vodou

The Ultimate Guide to an African Diasporic Religion and Its Influence on Louisiana Voodoo, Santería and Candomblé

© Copyright 2022

The content contained within this book may not be reproduced, duplicated, or transmitted without direct written permission from the author or the publisher.

Under no circumstances will any blame or legal responsibility be held against the publisher, or author, for any damages, reparation, or monetary loss due to the information contained within this book, either directly or indirectly.

Legal Notice:

This book is copyright protected. It is only for personal use. You cannot amend, distribute, sell, use, quote, or paraphrase any part, or the content within this book, without the consent of the author or publisher.

Disclaimer Notice:

Please note the information contained within this document is for educational and entertainment purposes only. All effort has been executed to present accurate, up-to-date, reliable, complete information. No warranties of any kind are declared or implied. Readers acknowledge that the author is not engaging in the rendering of legal, financial, medical, or professional advice. The content within this book has been derived from various sources. Please consult a licensed professional before attempting any techniques outlined in this book.

By reading this document, the reader agrees that under no circumstances is the author responsible for any losses, direct or indirect, that are incurred as a result of the use of the information contained within this document, including, but not limited to, errors, omissions, or inaccuracies.

Your Free Gift (only available for a limited time)

Thanks for getting this book! If you want to learn more about various spirituality topics, then join Mari Silva's community and get a free guided meditation MP3 for awakening your third eye. This guided meditation mp3 is designed to open and strengthen ones third eye so you can experience a higher state of consciousness. Simply visit the link below the image to get started.

https://spiritualityspot.com/meditation

Contents

INTRODUCTION	1
CHAPTER 1: INTRODUCTION TO VOODOO…OR VODOU?	4
Origin	5
The Role of Vodou	6
The Difference between Voodoo and Hoodoo	7
The Benefits and Power of Vodou	8
Working with a Vodouisant	9
CHAPTER 2: MAIN VODOU BELIEFS	11
Bondye	12
The Lwa	12
The Hounfo	13
The Altar	15
Practices and Rituals	16
Who's in a Sosyete?	17
The Vodou Ritual Calendar	17
Vodou Dancing, Drumming, and Rhythm	18
Difference between Haitian Lwa Possession and Biblical Demonic Possession	19
CHAPTER 3: WHO ARE BONDYE AND THE TWINS?	20
Bondye	20
The Lwa	22

Marassa Jumeaux, the Divine Twins	23
Serving the Marassa	25

CHAPTER 4: THE GENTLE ONES – RADA LWA 27

Legba	27
Loko	28
Ayizan	29
Damballah	30
Agwe	31
La Sirene	32
Ezili Freda	33
Filomez	34
Klemezin	35
Zaka	35
Ogou	36
Lwa Correspondences	37

CHAPTER 5: THE VIOLENT ONES – PETWO LWA 40

Ezili Danto	41
Kalfou	41
Bossou	42
Simbi	43
Gran Bwa	44
Igbo	45
Djabs	46
Maître Carrefour	47
Marinette	49
Don Petro	50
Lwa Correspondences	51

CHAPTER 6: THE MASTERS OF DEATH – GUEDE LWA 53

A Peculiar Group of Lwa	54
The Ancestors	59
Lwa Correspondences	59

CHAPTER 7: VODOU ALTARS AND DOLLS 61

About Your Altar	61
Before You Set Up Your Home Altar	63

- Another Way to Set Up an Ogantwa 65
- Setting Up Your Home Altar 67
- Tips on Making Vodou Altars 67
- Voodoo Dolls 69
- Making Your Vodou Doll 70
- How Vodou Dolls Work 71
- Properly Disposing of a Doll 71

CHAPTER 8: VODOU IN SANTERIA AND CANDOMBLE 72
- The Difference between Hoodoo, Vodou, and Santeria 72
- Vodou and Santeria 73
- Organization in Santeria 77
- The Priesthood in Santeria 78
- Divination 78
- Vodou and Candomble 78
- Is Voodoo Hoodoo? 79
- Racism and Stereotyping of African Traditional Religions 80

CHAPTER 9: VODOU FESTIVALS AND CELEBRATIONS 81
- List of Vodou Celebrations 82

CHAPTER 10: VODOU AS A WAY OF LIFE 92
- Can Anyone Practice Vodou? 94
- First Steps 94
- Are the Lwa Calling You? How Should You Respond? 95
- Finding a Mambo or Houngan to Do a Reading 96
- After Your Reading 98
- Finding the Right Vodou House for You 99
- Questions to Ask Before Joining a House 101

CONCLUSION 103

HERE'S ANOTHER BOOK BY MARI SILVA THAT YOU MIGHT LIKE 106

YOUR FREE GIFT (ONLY AVAILABLE FOR A LIMITED TIME) 107

REFERENCES 108

Introduction

If you've always been curious about Haitian Vodou, you've made an excellent choice by picking this book. Think of it like a very comprehensive handbook that tells you everything you need to know about the beliefs and main principles of the religion. You're going to discover how Haitian Vodou influenced Candomble, Santeria, and Louisiana Voodoo.

You might be completely new to this topic or pretty well-versed in it. Either way, this book will definitely add to your knowledge and give you a fresh perspective on practicing the religion's foundational principles. Unlike other books full of terms an average reader may struggle with, this is written clearly in plain English.

Many African Traditional Religions (ATRs) aren't common among contemporary Africans. Still, it's worth remembering that their ancestors were ripped from their homes, loves, and lives during one of the ugliest times in history, the Atlantic slave trade. These people were forced into strange lands, stripped of their dignity, and were compelled to work as slaves in the "New World." Somehow, Africans in several parts of this New World (like the Caribbean and Latin America) rescued whatever they could from their religious practices. They found comfort in their gods, who gave them a sense of serenity and strength in tumultuous, treacherous times.

There's so much more to Haitian Vodou than what you find on the internet. This book is written to fill the huge gap in knowledge on this deeply spiritual movement. So, you can rest assured that everything you get here is so much more than what you could find with a Google search.

You're going to get practical applications of practices and rituals explained step-by-step so that you don't miss any trick or detail you need to learn. By the time you're done reading this, you'll be able to perform the rituals with confidence and ease and will have a newfound respect for this way of life.

Every page of this book is fully packed with expert information, recorded in such a way that doesn't encourage cultural appropriation. You're getting an objective and thorough insight into Haitian Vodou's beliefs, history, and practices. You'll find yourself captivated by the connection between the Orishas, Lwa, and other important deities and how these deities are real influences in the lives of Vodou practitioners.

This book comes from a place of love and appreciation for this way of life. All things about Haitian Vodou must be maintained and preserved. Every philosophy and ritual of Vodou should be cherished and kept free from foreign influences that seek to change the religion. We must do our bit to keep it from becoming something that it's not and protect it from being ripped away from the original Vodou faith. This book ensures that the future generations of Vodouisants always have a reliable reference to fall back on to keep the uniqueness and richness of their culture alive.

The true follower of this path doesn't consider this way of life a fad or something to gain "cool points" with. They know that there's nothing to trifle with and are generally aware of much deeper meanings and implications of every step of every ritual. By the time you're finished with this book, you will find your practice is richer and more rewarding, spiritually and otherwise. If you're ready to connect with the Divine in a more fulfilling way than ever, you've made the right choice with this book.

Chapter 1: Introduction to Voodoo...or Vodou?

You may have wondered what the difference between Voodoo and Vodou might be, but there's none. Vodou is simply the Haitian spelling of Voodoo. Other spellings you may come across are Vodoun, Vodon, Vudu, Vundun, Vowdown, Vooodooo, etc. Vodou is a Fon word that describes a pantheon of deities revered by the people of West Africa. The Kreyol spelling also clearly distinguishes between Haitian Vodou and the derivatives of West African Vodou traditions, like New Orleans Voodoo.

Most Westerners think of magical dolls, incantations nor chants, and animal sacrifice when they hear the word "Vodou," but that's not it. Vodou, for practitioners from Haiti (Ayiti, meaning "mountain land" or "motherland") and the black diaspora in South America, the United States, and Africa, is about patron saints and ancestral spirits. Ayiti is the name given to the island by the peoples of Arawak and Taino. It was Christopher Columbus who renamed it Hispaniola to honor his patrons who were Spanish royalty.

Vodou practitioners used Vodou to resist the French colonial empire. Contrary to popular opinion derived from the media's depictions of rituals and magic, Vodou actually played a role as a health care system of sorts by offering religious healing.

Origin

Haitian Vodou was – of course – developed in Haiti. It's an African diasporic religion that arose through the syncretization of different spiritual schools of thought. Among these philosophies were Freemasonry, Roman Catholic Christianity, and traditional religions of Central and West Africa, particularly from those enslaved parts, among them Kongo, Fon, and Yoruba. These people were brought to Hispaniola, where they adopted the French colonialists' way of life in Saint-Domingue. This happened from the 16th to the 19th century. As a religion, it has no central authority to dictate its practice. It is also very diverse, as some practitioners are Serviteurs, Vodouists, Vodouisants, or, as the Kreyol spell it, Vodouwizan.

Vodou is centered on spirits called Lwa. These beings get their attributes and names from the Central and West African deities or divinities and are on par with the saints of Roman Catholicism. The Lwa are made up of two major groups: the Rada and the Petwo. Many stories and myths surround these beings, who, while revered, are subservient to Bondye, the Creator God.

This religion is both monotheistic and polytheistic. For initiations, the Vodouists come together in a temple called the *ounfo* in reverence for the Lwa. The ounfo is overseen by a mambo (priestess) or a houngan (priest). There's a main ritual where the practitioners sing, drum, and dance to invoke a Lwa to take over one of them and communicate through them whatever they need to know. The practitioners offer liquor, fruit, and sometimes animal sacrifices. They also give offerings to the spirits of those who have passed on. They practice different kinds of divination to figure out what the Lwa has to tell them. They work a lot with healing rituals and prepare talismans and herbal remedies.

The Role of Vodou

Many Vodouists were part of the Haitian Revolution which lasted from 1791 to 1804. Historians believed that religion was heavily influenced by slaves who had escaped and sought to light a fire in other slaves' hearts so that they would rebel. Vodou was the unifying spiritual force that spurred this revolution.

The revolution led to the overthrow of the French colonial government, abolishment of slavery, and transformation of Saint-Domingue into Haiti. After this time, the Roman Catholic Church left the region for decades, allowing Vodou to become the dominant religion of the Republic of Haiti.

From 1835 to 1987, the Haitian government attempted to ban Voodoo by making it illegal to carry out rituals. However, the Haitian government found it close to impossible to implement those laws. Therefore, by the 19th century, Voodoo was a central belief system that had covertly sunk its hooks into the elite culture. The elites couldn't risk showing their support for the movement in the open. The Roman Catholic Church had forced Haiti to take on Roman Catholicism as the nation's official religion.

Over the subsequent years, there were many campaigns launched by Protestant and Catholic churches against Voodoo, and even systematic attacks on Voodoo objects and temples were done for several decades. All this led to Voodoo being maligned as evil sorcery. Still, the Vodou flame continued to burn – thankfully.

By the 20th century, Vodou became more popular, thanks to emigration. The latter part of this century also saw more connections between Vodou and other traditions in the Americas and West Africa, like the Brazilian Candomble and the Cuban Santeria. The Negritude Movement also influenced some practitioners to the point where they actively wanted to eliminate all Roman Catholic marks on the religion.

Many Haitians are Vodouists to some degree while also being Roman Catholic. For them, there is no conflict in following both paths at the same time. Outside of Haiti, there are other smaller communities, particularly among the Haitian diaspora in America. This religion has spread like wildfire at home and abroad, drawing people of all ethnicities towards it.

The Difference between Voodoo and Hoodoo

These belief systems are totally different, even though they may seem the same. The major difference between them is that while Voodoo (Vodoun) is considered a religion, Hoodoo isn't.

Is Vodou Really a Religion?

We only refer to Vodou as a religion, for lack of a better word. It's more of a collection of practices that demonstrate certain beliefs, at least for those within Haiti. The country mostly has Protestants and Catholics (more of the latter), while most practice Vodou. They don't even call it Vodou often. Instead, they call it *sèvi lwa*, which means "serving the Lwa." it's a way of life that is related to the mo (ancestors) and the Lwa (family spirits).

Some Vodouisants are Catholic or Protestant – many are neither. The important thing for them is the belief in Divine Creator and subservient, non-human beings that the creator provided humanity to help one and all. Bondye is the Good God, also known as Gran Met, or the Great Master.

Why Vodou?

Thanks to Western influence and modern life, many African religions have slowly but surely lost their hold, but somehow, Vodou has remained tough. Despite its global bad rap, it still holds its own. Many practice Vodou because they were born into practicing families, so they are obligated to honor the Lwa from childhood. Some followers come to this practice much later in life, often the case with Haiti's urbanization and emigration to other countries. Some are called to service by a long-forgotten family Lwa, through visions, possessions at a ceremony, or a dream. Even non-Haitians are drawn to service more and more. It's not clear why, but the Lwa aren't bothered one bit about where you're from — and that's a good thing. As long as your service is rendered in truth and sincerity, you're welcome to practice.

Being pragmatic, Haitians serve the Lwa mostly for the benefits of doing so. These benefits include health, wealth, protection, favor, guidance, and spiritual wellbeing.

Haitians are almost like the Igbos of Eastern Nigeria. They have their family Chi and other deities common to Igbo culture. Haitians have the family Lwa they serve and the more commonly recognized Lwa. We'll get into further details as we move along in this book.

The Benefits and Power of Vodou

Say the word *Vodou*, and chances are you might get a negative response or at least a weird look from people. Sadly, Vodou has been unfairly maligned in the media. Movies have done a good job in making people believe that it's only about black magic and is only practiced by those who want to harm others. When you consider the evil zombie phenomena where victims under the influence of certain plants were rendered paralyzed and pliant, it's easy to dismiss Vodou quickly.

Many believe that every Vodou ritual is about punishing and hurting. Want to punish someone who has cheated on you with someone else? Hex them! Is someone getting ahead of you in life? Curse them! However, the real truth is that there's nothing as occult or scary about Vodou spells as you might assume. Most of the gruesome and lurid tales you hear are often exaggerated to the nth degree.

Having said that, Vodou magic is indeed powerful as it draws on the Lwa's abilities. These Vodoun gods have powers that you can use to execute your will. This is why many Vodouisants tell new practitioners to be careful in their spell casting because these spells often work well. In fact, you could argue that they work a little too well.

To put this simply, whenever you cast a Vodou spell for a target, you can rest assured you've bound that person's soul and cause to yours, and it will remain that way until the goal of the spell is fulfilled. Say you cast a love spell, for instance. You'd need to be absolutely sure that you're ready to be with that person because they will be yours indefinitely. You can see how that could become problematic if you were only infatuated with them and not actually in love. Eventually, you might get tired of them, but do what you can, to get rid of them, but it's not going to happen unless you work a spell to negate the first one you cast.

Working with a Vodouisant

So, any Vodouisant worth their salt will give you this clear warning: Only ever cast spells if you're absolutely ready for the results. This shouldn't put you off, though. As Peter Shankman puts it in his book, *Faster than Normal*, you don't have all your problems eradicated once you become rich or get that car or the lover you wished for. What you get instead is a *new set of problems*. For instance, if you don't have a home and want one, you have to be ready to pay bills, keep it clean, etc. Sure, right now you're dealing with the struggle of not having your own space; maybe you're ticked off your long-suffering friend with that depression you've left on their couch, but are you ready for the problems that come with being a homeowner? If your answer to that question is yes, then you're good to go. The point is that you should be careful what you wish for because you're going to get it.

A true Vodouisant will consider your happiness and welfare before their own desires. They won't just help you out with a spell that may not be what you need or won't serve your highest good. Knowing this, it should be even harder to reconcile that kind of personality with the ugly picture Hollywood and other media aspects want to paint of this practice. Vodou is not about causing anguish, suffering, misery, pain, and death. On the contrary, it's a practice that can make your life so much more worth it.

You need to be aware of the fact that Vodou is not something to be trifled with. If you want to cast spells to get back at someone, punish them, or bind them to you in love only to reject them, it would not be a wise decision. The Lwa aren't idiots; they are aware of your true intentions, so you can be sure that all cruel acts will be punished when the time is right. To avoid dealing with their wrath, it's best not to tick them off to begin with. The Lwa reward sincerity and honesty, but they aren't kind to those who think that Vodou is nothing but a joke.

Unfortunately, we live in times when people have no qualms about appropriating others' cultures. They claim just to be showing their "appreciation." Still, you don't have to look under the hood too long to know that they are only involved in Vodou because it's the "hot topic" at the moment. It may appear that they're getting away with it, but there's a common Nigerian saying, "Every day for the thief; one day for the owner." In other words, it's only a matter of time before the Lwa deals with disrespectful frauds.

Chapter 2: Main Vodou Beliefs

In this chapter, we'll go over the main beliefs of Haitian Vodou. Again, Haitians don't even call it Vodou in everyday lingo; the term just makes it easier to label the body of beliefs and practices. The Vodouisant is more likely to tell you that they're *houngan* or serve the Spirit or the Lwa.

These beliefs have been passed on through oral tradition. Even in this day and age, a considerable population of Haitians isn't literate. They don't write things down and have never had to. In fact, some lineages absolutely forbid writing certain concepts down. Vodouisants are very mindful about what they share, seeking permission from elder practitioners before divulging certain secrets.

That's the thing about Vodou; it's very unlike Judaism, Christianity, or Islam. It's not a revealed religion. There's no central tenet, no sacred book, no special creed for practicing Vodou. There is no such thing as "Vodou evangelism," where some sacred text is taught and explained to would-be followers of the way. It's a tradition steeped in practice, a cultic one like Buddhism. You gain experience through personal involvement in ceremonies, rituals, and your own practice. This is why many Vodouisants don't bother writing things down and would instead invite you to take part or show you by themselves.

Regardless of this, we can talk about the structure of Vodou. To be clear, there are variations from place to place and even among families and lineages in the same space. Still, some things remain constant, regardless; let's talk about them now.

Bondye

Haitian Vodou is monotheistic, with a Divine Creator who is mostly impersonal. This God is at the center of Vodou and is known as Bondye, which means "Good God." Bondye is the one who made the universe and continues to maintain it each day. The Bondye is similar to God, the Father, according to Roman Catholic views. This being is more focused on keeping the universe running as it should and less concerned with the mundane lives of humanity.

Most Vodouisants consider the Christian God and Bondye to be the same being. They start each ceremony by praying to Bondye. Other rituals and liturgical work dedicated to spirits or ancestors are done after this prayer, or as they say, "apres Bondye."

To be clear, Bondye is the epitome of universal order and the truest, purest form of love. This supreme entity handles all matters of destiny and fate. Mambos or houngans draw power by invoking all kinds of powers and spirits at will. Still, the only reason their magic works is because Bondye allows it, or as the Haitians say, *Si Bondye vle*, meaning, "God wills it." All other beings and powers must bow before Bondye's will. Nothing can change the universe without Bondye granting that request.

The Lwa

While Vodou is a monotheistic religion, it could also be called polytheistic because of lesser spirits or gods who are also Bondye's creation. They are known as the Lwa (or Loa). Some would argue that the system of beliefs isn't particularly monotheistic but a flexible form of polytheism or henotheism, where there's a hierarchy of several divine beings. Others call it a monolatry, as in a kind of henotheism where the "lesser" beings are simply different personalized aspects of the more abstract Creator.

The relationship between the Lwa and humans involves reciprocity. As a believer, you provide offerings of food and other things that the Lwa enjoy, and in exchange, they grant you whatever you need. They are usually invited to take over or possess a Vodouisant during rituals so that the others in the family or community can connect with them directly.

Vilokan is home to the Lwa and those who have passed on. It's usually described as a forested, submerged island guarded by a being called the Lwa Legba. Before one can speak to the other residents of this place, they must appease Legba or Papa Legba.

The Hounfo

This practice has no central authority to organize it and no scripture to dictate its practice. There are no basic standards that tell you the proper way to perform each rite, yet there is some guidance in the form of the regleman. These are simple guidelines on how to serve each Lwa, the correct order to address them. They also include other specific details about events and ceremonies that need to be done for different reasons like initiation rituals or other rites of passage.

Like all the beliefs that make up Haitian Vodou, there's a Vodou priesthood made up of the initiated. The houngans are male priests, while the mambos are female. There's also a regleman of how these priests are ordained and trained. There's also a prescribed training course for those who want to be part of sosyetes but may not be a part of the priesthood.

Haitian Vodou is anything but solitary. There are some things you do in service of Bondye and the Lwa. Still, for the most part, service is carried out in the community, along with your sosyete or family. It can also be done in large groups with other sosyetes and families, in addition to yours.

The hounfo is a temple where Vodouisants come together to do ceremonies and serve the Lwa. It's a building or a group of buildings within a compound with a *peristil*, a clear space that's rather large. It's named "peristil" after the entryway of columns that you find in a classical temple or sanctuary. It could be circular, or more commonly, a rectangle or square. Here, the people dance and sing for the Lwa. You can find many buildings made up of just a room and a roof in this place. Some are in forests or grove openings, while others are like tents or huge roofs on columns. The latter sort is called a tonelle.

Each peristil or tonelle has a pole in the middle, or if it's outdoors, it has a tree in the center. The tree or pole is known as the *potomitan*, which means "middle pole." It's the very soul and center of Vodou ceremonies. All dances and ceremonies are done around this pole. The base of the pole is often fixed in concrete and decorated as an altar. The Lwa come down the pole from the heavens, landing on the peristil's floor. Then they rise up through the bodies of the faithful to dance with them or make their presence known through possessions.

The potomitan are usually decorated with depictions of two snakes intertwined. One of them represents Danbala-Wedo, while the other represents Ayida-Wedo. They both are responsible for holding the sky in place. Some poles could also be decorated with abstract, stripe-like patterns.

In larger hounfos, you can find other rooms that branch off from the peristil or more rooms or houses in the compound meant for other purposes. For instance, the *badji* is a room with an altar dedicated to a specific group of sports. You have one for the Petro badji, another for the Rada badji, and sometimes a third room for the Guede Lwa. In smaller houses, there may be no more than two rooms in the whole peristil. If there's just one room, all altars for these spirits will be set up to keep the families of these beings separate. If there are two rooms, the Guede will be outside them.

Sometimes, the Rada badji rooms can be used for initiation rites. At the same time, other sosyetes would rather have a *djevo*, a separate room for this purpose. Some hounfos have special rooms for Vodouisants to sleep overnight to gain answers from the Lwa through their dreams. There is also a residential area for the family who owns the hounfo and special rooms for herbal treatments, divinations, and other consultations. The smaller hounfos could either rent space for larger events or have their djevo, peristil, and altar in the same location.

The Altar

Calvin Hennick, for WBUR Boston, CC BY 3.0
https://creativecommons.org/licenses/by/3.0 via Wikimedia Commons
https://commons.wikimedia.org/wiki/File:Haitian_vodou_altar_to_Petwo,_Rada,_and_Gede_spirits;_November_5,_2010..jpg

The altars in Haitian Vodou are very striking and not always a pretty sight. Most of them aren't any different from plain old tables. On them, you can find interesting items from bowls, plates, cups, pieces of ribbon, cloth, weaponry, stones, and roots, to pictures of the saints, candles, flowers, food, all kinds of bottles, oil lamps, water goblets, and every now and then, a human skull. These things may seem completely random to the non-practitioner, but a true Vodouisant knows with just a glance which spirit the altar is meant for and how the spirit should be served.

On the altar, there are favorite offerings of a particular Lwa. There's also a wall peg for a dress they put on if they enter the peristil in possession.

Let's talk about Legba's altar, for instance. You'll usually find a straw bag on top of it or hanging from a tree branch close to the bodji. Simbi-Dlo, Lasiren, or other watery Lwa might ask for basins of water on their altars or nearby. Ezili Freda loves to have wedding rings on the altar you set up for her. Ezili Danto asks for a baby doll for her viewing pleasure and a dagger to use for protection.

Many of these altars are permanent. Some are set up for specific ceremonies or treatments, and some can be moved around. For instance, you have the Lwa Met Agwe ceremony, also known as the Maje Me or "feeding the sea." The altar here has the offerings and colors favored by Agwe and is taken out to sea on a boat. It's then thrown into the ocean when the boat is pretty far off from the land, and the waves carry that altar away.

Practices and Rituals

Since there's no standardization per se, it's not easy to capture every belief of every Vodouiosant. For instance, some families have their own Lwa, veves, or Catholic saints. When it comes to Vodou rituals, there could be animal sacrifice depending on which Lwa the believers are reaching out to. These sacrifices are a form of sustenance for the Lwa, spiritually speaking. The animal's flesh is then cooked as a meal and shared for participants to enjoy.

In rituals, it's the norm to draw specific symbols known as veves using cornmeal or any other powder. Every Lwa has its own symbol; some of them have more than one each. What about Vodou dolls?

What relevance do they have? To be clear, that image you may have in your head of Vodouisants sticking pins into dolls isn't a true or clear reflection of traditional Vodou. Having said that, they do dedicate dolls to certain Lwa to draw their power and influence. Think Ezeli Danto.

Who's in a Sosyete?

The sosyete comprises the mambo and houngan, the *ounsi* or "children of the spirits," and the *ountogi* or ritual drummers. They share their knowledge through initiation rituals known as kanzo, where the body is the literal site of spiritual change. You will find that there are variations in hierarchies and practices all over Haiti. Some branches of Vodou include Ibo, Daome, Rada, Petwo, Manding, Dereal, and Kongo. You will not find a specific leader or someone you can call a spokesperson. Still, the different groups occasionally try to set up some organizational structures.

Other than the usual societies, secret ones (known as Sanpwel or Bizango) serve judicial-religious purposes.

The Vodou Ritual Calendar

A calendar of feasts gives Vodou an annual rhythm, syncretized with that of the Roman Catholics'. Major days dedicated to Lwa are celebrated on the same days as Roman Catholic saints; for instance, you celebrate Ogou on July 25, the same as Saint James's day. Ezeli Danto is celebrated on July 16, a day sacred to Our Lady of Mount Carmel. On March 17, Saint Patrick's day, Vodouisants celebrate Danbala. They celebrate their ancestors on 1st and 2nd November, being All Saints' Day and All Souls' Day, respectively.

Other feasts are for the poor, for sacred children, and specific ancestors. You also have funerary and initiation rituals that take place all through the year.

Vodou Dancing, Drumming, and Rhythm

Drumming, dancing, and rhythm are inextricably linked to Vodou and practiced faithfully. The essence of drumming rituals is to draw down the ancestral spirits and Lwa to offer the faithful their instruction, assistance, strengths, and special powers. Drumming helps the people invoke the Lwa to allow them to embody their unique characteristics and principles.

To become a drummer, you have to partake in a very long apprenticeship. The rhythm, drumming style, and orchestral composition can vary depending on the Lwa being invoked. The rhythms of the drums will usually create a break called *kase*, which the main drummer begins to serve as a counterpoint to the main rhythm which the other drummers play. This causes a sense of destabilization for the dancers, thereby putting them in a better position to become possessed by the Lwa.

In addition to drumming, there's singing, often done in Haitian Creole or Kreyol. The songs are sung in a call and response format. A soloist sings one line and everyone else choruses the same line or a different, shorter version. The solo singer is called the *hungenikon* and is responsible for keeping the rhythm using a rattle. The songs sung at rituals are simple, repetitive, and perfect for summoning any of the Lwa.

Dancing is equally important in Vodou rituals. You see, the dances are very simple, as there's no sophisticated choreography involved. Often, the dancers move around the potomitan counterclockwise. There are certain dances meant to summon specific Lwa and Lwa families. For instance, it's easy to spot dances meant to summon Agwe, as they're reminiscent of swimming. For Vodouisants, the Lwa can renew themselves through the dancers' vitality and vigor.

Difference between Haitian Lwa Possession and Biblical Demonic Possession

You may have wondered a few times already about the idea of being possessed in Haitian Vodou. There's no reason to let that scare you away from the practice because it's absolutely nothing like in the movies or Christianity. In fact, this possession by the Lwa allows the Vodouisant to live a life of joy and happiness. Through this process, they have a visceral and real connection with their Lwa, not depending on blind faith alone as in Christianity.

Some argue that Lwa possessions are actual demonic encounters, but there is simply no truth to that. In Biblical demonic possessions, the possessed person often winds up being insane or ill in some way. They're often tormented by the demonic beings that possess them. Another interesting thing about Biblical possessions is that the possessed person takes on a completely new personality who controls every aspect of them. The person is no longer home in their body, so to speak. The personality will use different names and pronouns than whoever they possess, be given immorality, afflict the body they're in with convulsions and seizures, and manifest as physical illnesses. Also, there is absolutely nothing voluntary about these possessions. The possessed person does not ask to be taken over.

When it comes to Lwa possessions, the possessed person does have a different personality in control. Still, they act rationally and often the same way the Lwa would act. Each Lwa has its own preferences, mannerisms, and physical attributes, so the possessed person takes on those traits. Everyone around them would know immediately that the Lwa is present.

Also, in the state of possession by a Lwa, the Vodouisant may suddenly have clairvoyant abilities and extraordinary strength. However, at no point are any demons involved in the process. The Lwa are created by Bondye, whose name implies goodness and purity, qualities that are the complete antithesis of all things demonic.

Chapter 3: Who Are Bondye and the Twins?

Bondye

As mentioned, Bondye is French for "good God," the Creator, much like the Christian God. Vodouisants rarely reach out to this being for help directly; instead, they connect to the Lwa or Loa. The Lwa are the entities that Bondye expresses his power through. Bondye is connected to all of life and the Haitian community. So, the Vodouisants come together to celebrate religious ceremonies full of vibrant energy to honor this God better.

A distant, mysterious figure, Bondye is the main spiritual head of the Barons of Bondye Chapter. Followers of Bondye are known as Vodouisants, as this God is at the center of all Vodou spirituality. He is the highest principle in all creation, making sure that life is as it should be. While he's called "the good god," there's no equal but opposite force to him. A metric for goodness in Vodou is the level of repression or expression of Bondye's power in the world based on our actions. So, prosperity, freedom, health, and happiness are good, while anything that threatens these things is bad.

Bondye is beyond understanding for us humans, and that's why it's not easy to interact with him directly. It's much better to connect with the Lwa he created; these are spirits that show up as forces that influence our daily lives. All Vodou ceremonies focus on the Lwa and never Bondye. The latter has never possessed a Vodouisant in the same way as the Lwa.

Some people say that the Lwa are gods and goddesses of various aspects of life: Legba being in charge of the crossroads, Freda the love goddess, and so on. However, Vodouisants know that this is blasphemy. Bondye is the one true God. The Lwa, saints, and angels are all his servants and nothing more. He uses them to express himself to the people, but they are not equal to him. Bondye made them, and when he was done with creating the world, he handed its care over to the Lwa, saints, and angels. Bondye is not to be approached, but he has set these beings to protect us from all harm.

Some say that this idea is a result of Christianity's corrupting influence over the real African traditions. However, many African cultures have legends of a creator goddess or God who crafted the world and left its operations to spirits. These spirits were subservient to the one true God while being more knowledgeable and powerful than all humans combined. So, the Creator is to be revered and honored. Still, more attention is given to the spirits closer to the physical world. Among the Lwa are heroes who passed to the other side, ancestors, plant spirits, and totem animals charged with reward and punishing those who follow them.

If it helps, you could think of Bondye as the Horned God, the Universal Mother, the Absolute and Eternal, or the Great Divinity. These are all just terms that attempt to help our minds understand the unknowable — an impossible feat, by the way.

Vodouisants don't bother too much about the metaphysics of Vodou, as they experience real, practical results from their service to the Lwa. Very few houngans and mambos could be bothered to get into theoretical arguments about such irrelevant things. They know that the relationship they have with these beings and their continued devotion is more important.

The Lwa

The Lwa are organized in families called *nanchons,* and the common ones are Rada, Petwo, and Guede or Ghede or Gede. Some spirits don't fit into any of those categories, or they may appear in several pantheons but in various forms. They are the *miste,* meaning "mysteries," because they can't be understood from a purely logical standpoint and can't be neatly packaged into boxes. As they are beyond complete comprehension, how much more difficult it must be then to understand the great Bondye or speak definitively about him.

It's common practice for Vodouisants to make their offerings to the Lwa. The latter then possess them to interact directly with the rest of the community. It's easy to assume the Lwa as gods, but this couldn't be further from the truth. They are spiritual intermediaries between the physical world and the Divine Creator, Bondye.

Many newcomers or those who do not understand Vodou tend to focus more on the Lwa being gods. They don't pay much attention to Bondye because he seems irrelevant and distant. However, you shouldn't make this mistake.

A good way to understand the Lwa is to think of them as Bondye's extensions, but also different from Bondye. It's the same thing with Christianity. You have Jehovah (the main God) and other names. For instance, Jehovah Jireh (the Lord that provides), Jehovah Nissi, Jehovah Rapha (the Lord that heals), El Elyon (the highest God), and so on. Neither of these names is another God but part of the same singular God. In the Western world, particularly America, it's as though the Vodouisants are leaning towards atheism. However, true Vodouisants acknowledge Bondye in all things. They simply accept the Lwa as Bondye's servants who personify aspects of him to make it easier for the faithful to interact with Great Divinity.

Since the Vodouisants don't think of the Lwa as God, they are fine with bargaining. The way they see it, they offer their service to the spirits, and therefore the spirits should offer their service in return. They're not afraid to let a Lwa know that their demands cannot be met in the moment or offer something else in return for whatever the spirits want. They're not afraid to let the Lwa know that they will simply stop their service if they don't acquiesce to their requests. This doesn't mean they aren't respectful to these beings; it just means that Vodouisants know that they can and should set boundaries with them. So, never assume that you must come to the Lwa in fear and trepidation. You definitely don't need to let them enslave you. You should know that you have the right to expect them to help you in exchange for your veneration.

Marassa Jumeaux, the Divine Twins

More ancient than the Lwa, *Marassa Jumeaux* are the divine twins. Often syncretized with Saints Damian and Cosmas, these children play a prominent role in Vodou. They are all about justice, truth, love, and reason. All mysteries concerning the connection of heaven and earth are embodied in them.

These twins are different from the Lwa. They are above the Lwa, and while being twins, they are also three in number — male and female, and both male and female. It's very interesting to see the concept of divine dichotomy represented in Haitian Vodou in this way. In some houses, they are served right after Legba instead of being channeled through ritual possession.

The Marassa received lots of attention from scholars in the first half of the 20th century. As it shares similar ties with twin cults in Africa, devotion to these twins proved the survival of these old practices from Africa in the Americas. They are vital in the religious lives of those who practice Vodou, especially practitioners who are twins, triplets, or from families with unusual or multiple births.

Sometimes depicted as conjoined twins, they serve by Legba's side. Legba is the deity of the crossroads connecting humanity with divinity. He also acts as the voice of Bondye.

The Marassa twins embody faith, hope, and charity, otherwise known as the three virtues. They can be childish to the extreme. They love food and always eat till they're satisfied, only to complain that they haven't eaten yet. They love to play games and love toys as well. When they're angry, they can be very irrational and resort to the cruelest punishments. For the most part, Vodouisants avoid getting on their bad side as they can be very sensitive and throw terrible tantrums.

It is important to treat each twin the same way so that neither feels slighted or jealous of the other. Set their offerings on similar banana leaves or plates on the floor. This way, they can enjoy the food with their hands and at their leisure, like kids. You should also never offer them vegetables, as veggies are insulting and can destroy their abilities. Altars dedicated to them will have two dolls on them. It's important to respect the schedule you have for them to avoid the consequences of their tantrums.

Offerings made to these twins include little dolls, popcorn, and candy. Honoring the twins requires double the work to remind the practitioner that the twins can bring you two times more of whatever you seek. They give good luck, heal people, bring the rain, have clairvoyant abilities, and a special ability to double or triple anything. Triplets, twins, or those who have extra appendages are connected to the twins. They're considered naturally mystical and more connected to the Lwa. Why are people with extra appendages added to the mix? It's believed that the extra appendage belongs to a twin that the person "ate" while in the womb.

The twins represent the idea of one plus one being equal to three. They are also called Marassa Dosu Dosa to depict the idea that "two is three." They represent the gift of children, blessings, abundance, and the sacredness of the family unit. They also represent children born with cauls on their faces.

Without these twins, nothing can happen or exist. They have mafic that causes the world as we know it to be. They are also syncretized with the Three Egyptians or Virtues in Petro service. They are identical, sexless, and therefore embody all energies, light and dark, male and female, negative and positive.

Serving the Marassa

These divine twins ensure that everything we desire is manifested in our lives, not once but over and over again. The Marassa, while being two or three, is truly beyond the idea of numbers. They are also the manifestation of the Dosu Dosa, the first child born right after the twins. They can show up in any number they want. The Marassa Twa are the Divine Triplets that are at Papa Marassa's feet.

These beings can show up in both Petro and Rada guides. In Rada, they are part of Papa Loko's escorts. While they show up in their Petro form in green and red, green and yellow are the colors that are used to serve them.

When parents have twins, they are thought lucky and given the honorary titles Manman Gimo and Papa gizmo, which means Mama and Papa Marassa. The twins come to you as true children. When they have possessed a Vodouisant, they will usually cry and laugh, eat food from the *laye (a wooden plate on which offerings are served)* and toss it all around. They act like kids and love nothing more than having other children around. Cute as this might sound, you should never think little of them or their power, wisdom, and knowledge. They are especially gifted healers.

In Rada, the Marassa are honored on Thursday; in Petro, they are honored on Tuesday. Saturday is also a good day to serve them. When at the fet, they are offered a laye, a woven plate with cookies, candy, popcorn, bonbon sirop, fruit soda, and peanuts. There are also special criche (serving vessels) used to serve these beings, having two or three pots made of earthenware that are clay cups connected to one another. Food goes into the base of the criche while the pots are filled with water.

You can also offer the Marassa toys, marbles, and other things children enjoy. Make sure that every item is the same in shape, size, color, and so on. Some practitioners get a reading to discover if they're dealing with the Marassa Jumeaux or the Marassa Twa so that they know if every offering needs to be made in twos or threes.

In your service, deal with them with the spirit of fun and play. They may be very powerful and the most ancient of spirits, but they're also children at heart. So, deal with them as you would with regular kids - with joy and play in your heart. The Marassa are patrons of surgeons, physicians, herbalists, and pharmacists. The days to celebrate them are July 1, September 26, and October 17.

Chapter 4: The Gentle Ones — Rada Lwa

Vodouisants say that the Rada Lwa moves slower in pace than other spirits. They don't act as quickly as the Petwo. They're not as accessible as the Guede, yet this detachment makes it possible for them to see the entire picture and make wise decisions.

Doing the right thing means that their actions will definitely take some time, but the results will last longer and most likely change your life. You could also say that it's easier to seek them out than the hotter entities. Another interesting thing about them is that they will act with such speed and decisiveness every now and then; it will rock your world. Now let's take a look at each one.

Legba

Legba resembles an old man, seemingly unassuming, with a cane to support him as he limps along his way with his loyal dogs by his sides. He also has a corncob pipe, shabby clothes, and a straw bag. You might assume that he's a beggar, but he's far from that. The thing about Legba is that he can be rather deceptive with his looks. The cane he leans on is the bridge between Earth and heaven called the

P*oteau Mitan* (same as the potomitan). This is the way the Lwa can join ceremonies on Earth.

The only reason Legba limps is that he has each foot in different worlds — the physical and the spiritual. While he appears frail, he can cause even the best of plans to fail and take the lowest of the low to heights unimaginable.

At every ceremony, he is hailed first as he keeps the gateway, making sure that no one goes into the peristil without seeking his permission. As he knows every language on Earth and in heaven, he takes our messages to Bondye and the rest of the Lwa and brings their answers back to us. He's also a trickster with a fondness for paradox, riddles, and ambiguity. This is evident when it comes to the messages from the spirit realm, knowing that there's a huge chance they will be misinterpreted. He rules uncertainty and destiny at the same time.

Some honor Legba with white and red or red and black. Others use a yellow scarf. His followers insist on paying homage on Wednesday (or Monday or Tuesday, depending on who you ask). He loves grilled corn, peanuts, black coffee, tobacco for his pipe, palm oil, cane syrup, salt cod, plantains, yams, rum, gin, and cassava bread. It's a good idea to add a generous amount of cayenne to his food.

Loko

Loko was a royal ancestor, a spirit who was served by the priest-kings alone. He guards the peristil. He is the one who shared the secrets of healing by using leaves, trees, and herbs. He is the one who bestows the *asogwe* grade. All priests and priestesses who want to be at that grade have to head to the sacred ground or the demambwe to receive the asson (a ritual rattle) from Loko himself. Loko is particular about keeping the traditional ways and can get violent when traditions aren't respected.

This Lwa is syncretized with the father of Jesus, Saint Joseph. He is celebrated with a feast on March 19. His colors are harvest gold and white, he receives rice or a white rooster, and his food is usually kept in a ceiba tree.

Loko is a wonderful teacher, but his teachings are only for initiates introduced to him by others he has met already. If you haven't met him, he has nothing to do with you, so there's no reason to ask him for help. At best, you'll get no answer, and at worst, he might think you're arrogant and presumptuous.

It's different if you want to become a part of a sosyete or learn from a mambo or houngan. In this case, you can light a white or gold candle to Loko. If you want to, you can decorate your glass chimney with a photo of Saint Joseph or Loko's veve.

Ayizan

Ayizan is the very first mambo. She is in charge of the *kouche* along with Loko, leading the initiation or initiation ceremony. She makes sure that all ancestral knowledge passes from one generation to the next. She is syncretized with Saint Ann and can be represented by the Chire Ayizan or her veve. Her colors are silver and white, according to some followers. Others say it's white and gold or canary yellow and white. You can offer her palm hearts, bananas, and boiled white yams.

Mambo Ayizan can be approached by those who aren't initiated for help. She's the patroness of the market, and every woman with a small business can ask for her protection just by burning a white candle and offering her dates or palm hearts. As she's elderly, she doesn't act fast, but she is very protective and maternal, so you'll definitely get her blessings. The gifts she bestows may be subtle, but they are extremely powerful.

If you want a teacher to help you become an initiate, houngan, or mambo, you can ask her for help as well; light a yellow candle for

Loko and a white one for Ayizan. Ask them both to take care of you, and they'll make sure you get the very best in spiritual enlightenment.

Damballah

Damballah Wedo is one of the most powerful and honored of the Lwa. He is the great white python whose form encompasses the whole world, with 3,5000 coils of its body supporting the heavens and 3,500 coils beneath, holding up the Earth. The mountains are its dung, it is said. The Serpent is not a fan of heat. This is why we have the oceans in which it remained since the dawn of time, feeding on iron bars delivered to it by red submarine monkeys. When the monkeys run out of iron, the Serpent will rise and writhe till the world falls into the sea and creation is destroyed. Some say the Serpent is in the sky, and it comes visiting after rainfall, taking the form of a rainbow.

As the images of Saint Patrick used to have snakes (because he had pursued the creatures out of Ireland), this saint became syncretized with Damballah. Damballah is therefore honored on March 17, also Saint Patrick's day.

Damballah loves cleanliness and purity, hates the smell of burning tobacco and alcohol, and would rather have all those saluting him put out their cigarettes and close all open containers. He loves to drink orgeat syrup, which is made from sugar and almonds. His color is snow white. As he was part of the ocean, and large snakes love wet places, the peristil usually has a large, shallow bowl of water for him. He's not a fan of blood — neither the sight nor the smell. If he's offered an animal, it's simply shown to him and then taken elsewhere to be killed.

This Lwa is the richest of them all and can help you deal with money troubles, but you need to offer him something you truly value, or else he might ignore you. However, if you're at the very end of your rope financially and you have no time to wait, he might have mercy on you and help you. He is compassionate and doesn't like his followers to suffer. Always thank him for his help, respect, and revere him in all your ways.

Agwe

Agwe or Met Agwe is a root Iwa, a very merciful and cool spirit capable of great wrath. He's an admiral, often dressed in naval uniform. He could be white, black, or mulatto. His eyes can be green or some other color. Some say that Agwe is female, but he's androgynous. He also shows up as various sea creatures and is syncretized with Saint.

When possessed by Agwe, the believer sits on a small chair as though they're on a boat. They are given a cane or a stick to use as a paddle. Then they'll paddle all around the room and pour water on themselves because Agwe loves being wet. If the religious ritual is happening on the boat or beach, the possessed believer may attempt to swim off, or they'll dive and come back up with a fish in hand. Agwe never speaks through them, but some Vodouisants hear him when he shows up. That's how they know what he wants from the community.

Agwe is offered cake with solver, white, green, and/or blue icing, white rice, white candles, liqueurs, champagnes, and a white sheep with its fleece dyed to match the blue of the sea. These are all set on a wooden raft, taken to the sea, and cast overboard.

On his altar are images or models of boats, which can be decorated with *Imamou*. His altar could also hold a paddle or an oar, netting, driftwood, and other sea artifacts, and you can also put conch shells and other seashells on it. To represent Agwe, followers use a Saint Ulrique lithograph.

Agwe loves things to be done the right way, all the time. He would rather you took your time setting up just one well-done service than have several cheap and careless ones done all the time. He opts for the good stuff, never scrimping or settling for cheap. He's also particular about cleanliness, like Damballah, but he's fine with alcohol. However, you should not smoke around him as he is a white Lwa. He rules the waters of the world, the ocean, and its vast treasures, so you need to connect with him sincerely as you would with a friend while giving him due respect.

He's a wealthy Lwa, very generous, and always ready to help you out when you're in need. If you treat him right and respect him, he will give you all you need and care for you. If you're struggling with money, light a green, blue, or white candle for him. Pour him some very nice liqueur — cordial, if you have it. Let him know you're having money issues and ask for his help. You can offer him a nice conch horn, stature, or flowers if he helps you out. While he has no use or need for your gifts, he will appreciate your good manners.

La Sirene

La Sirene is a mermaid who loves hard and, at the same time, cruel. She has wealth, beautiful hair, and a haunting voice. She carries a mirror in one hand and a comb in the other. It's said that she "walks on both roads." She can bring good fortune and luck when she is in her Rada aspect, but her Petwo form leads people to drown.

Those possessed by this Lwa will drop to the ground and swim or mime blowing a horn. They might take a seat and begin combing their hair or perform whirls on their toes like ballerinas. This Lwa doesn't speak but sings instead. She is different from Yemoja, the sea mother of Yoruba culture. The latter is connected to children and fertility and is a tender mother. La Sirene is the ultimate seductress who will grant you what you seek, but you must be careful about how you approach her and not assume that she's someone else.

La Sirene loves sweet things like cakes with light bluish-green and white icing. She never eats them, though; they're just pretty to look at. Also, she loves celebrations and parties — bonus points if you hold them in her honor. You can offer her liqueurs, orgeat syrup, or champagne. Leave these offerings on her shrine or at the beach. If you're going with the shrine, please take the offerings off them before they start to go bad, put them in a clean trash bag and toss them right away.

This is the Lwa to reach out to when you want to be more charming, improve your music, make better art, or do creative work. Just like a light blue, light green, or white, seven-day candle, set it in her crystal bowl, and ask her to help you. Always put a saucer between the candle and the crystal so that you don't crack the latter.

Ezili Freda

Ezili Freda is a Lwa to be respected. She can grant you favors when she loves you but can quickly be enraged when she feels offended, spurned, or neglected. A lovely mulatto woman, when she possesses the faithful, they apply powder and makeup on their faces and wear an outfit meant for her. They may also speak French, even when they don't know how to.

She is married to a bold warrior, Ogui Ferraille; the lord of the ocean, Agwe; and the wise white Serpent, Damballah. She's more like a mistress to each one than a wife. Agwe's main partner is La Sirene, Damballah's is Ayida Wedo, and Ogou's is Freda's sister, Ezili Danto.

Her best colors are baby pink and white. She loves pink roses, sweet things, lovely clothing, makeup, and jewelry and is the Lwa of luxury. Note that she is very jealous and doesn't like to be served along with others. So, you should pay her special attention rather than rattling off her name as just one of many goddesses in your practice.

Meditate next to her altar, tell her she's beautiful and you love her. Be sincere in your praise. You can also tell her about your problems and ask her for advice. Never compel her to do things for you. Instead, trust that she will show you her kindness and generosity and bless you with uncanny luck. Her devotees who go to a new country find a great place in a matter of hours in the right neighborhood at less than the going rate with a well-paying job.

If Freda wants something in particular and you can't make it happen, just tell her you will do it if she provides the means for you. You can bargain with her, but you must always keep up your end. She doesn't forget even if you forget her, and you don't want to witness her anger. When working with her, never give her anything black. You should never engage in sex right before her shrine, so don't place the shrine in or around your room if you can. Being a jealous Lwa, she might ruin your relationship if you make her watch. Some Vodouisants set a screen up between the altar and their bed when they don't have anywhere else that could work. Also, her shrine should never be beside the ones dedicated to the gods of the dead or the ancestors. She's not a fan of the Guede because they're foul-mouthed and represent death. Never smoke marijuana or cigarettes around her shrine as she dislikes the smell of burning. Work with Freda to be more attractive, look your best, be more charming, or make others love you. However, ask some other Lwa for help with getting you a lover because she's a hopeless romantic who believes love should always prevail. This sounds like a good thing until she brings you a bombshell model who drinks and spends too much or a talented sculptor who isn't doing great financially.

Filomez

Vodouisants serve this Lwa by using scarves of pastel colors, especially pale green, light yellow, light pink, and light blue. When she shows up, she'll dance all over the place through the possessed believer while scattering the bouquet of flowers given to her. Some claim she's a joyous merchant who gives prosperity to those who ask. Others see her more like Ezeli Freda's sister and the best Lwa to reach out to for matters of the heart. She is syncretized with Saint Philomena. Make sure you offer her fresh flowers like light yellow carnations, pink roses, or others in pastel shades before asking for her help.

Klemezin

Klemezin is known for getting rid of bad luck and negativity. She is served with white and light blue scarves and saluted with perfume and flower petals sprinkled on the floor. This is the Lwa to petition when you want clear dreams and clear vision. You can make her an offering of white flower petals, shredded coconut, and coconut water, all within a bowl of spring water. Set this beneath your bed, say Vodouisants, and Klemezin will give you all the insight and clarity you need to help you sort out your problems. Just make sure your place is clean before you do this.

You can offer her sweet, light blue or white cakes, as well as flowers in the same color. She also accepts perfumes. Other ways to honor her are to give charity on thanksgiving. If you work with this Lwa, you'll notice that you have an uncanny knack for spotting clear and obvious fixes to complex problems. Your intuition and instinct will always be spot on. This Lwa is syncretized with Saint Claire of Assisi.

Zaka

Zaka is a name answered by several spirits. For instance, you have Zaka Mini, the agriculture minister who takes himself so seriously that it's hilarious. There's Zaka Krebs, whose followers celebrate with an Indian war call; he is offered a burning stick to let him burn off the sores on his feet. Then there's Zaka Mede, an old man who simply sits on the floor when he shows up.

Some erroneously assume that he is a fertility spirit who helps the growth of wildlife and such, but he's really an agriculture spirit. He is all about working with the Earth and using it to achieve whatever you want or need. In other words, his gifts do not come without hard work, which he expects you to reward with gifts. His colors are dark green and dark blue, and you can light seven-day candles of either color to him or give him scarves or bandanas. He is syncretized with

Saint Isadore, another poor farmer who, like Zaka, wears rugged blue jeans and often prays in his field.

Zaka loves chaka, tripe, chayote, corn, and coconut. He will also eat rice and red beans, or anything else you make him; even if he doesn't like the meal, he's not picky when it comes to food, just like those who grew up poor aren't either. Never taste whatever you are about to serve him, or he will consider you a thief. He might refuse to eat, or he'll cause you to become terribly ill. Never use silverware to serve him and prepare his meals with a wooden spoon.

Ogou

Ogou is the first blacksmith, warrior, and hunter. He is also the first founder of dynasties and clearer of fields. Called Ogun in Yoruba, he defends and shields innocents who are unable to protect themselves. However, when he gets into a blind rage, he's quick to slaughter those who anger him. His color is red, the same as rust, hot iron, and dried blood. This Lwa is served with red scarves, but you can go for blue or white ones if you sense he'd like those. Wednesday is his day, so Vodouisants begin that morning by banging Ogun's machete on hard surfaces to get his attention. Then they'll pour a bit of rum into an iron cauldron or plate for him.

They set the rum on fire, run their hands through the burning flame so they can use it to slap their arms. While doing this, they ask the Lwa to give them courage and strength. It sounds risky, so please don't try this. The last thing he wants is you burning yourself or your home trying to serve him.

Turn to this Lwa if you're in a threatening situation or dealing with a dangerous person. Vodou doesn't care for the Wiccan idea, "and it harms none," so it's perfectly fine to ask Ogun to avenge you if someone has done you wrong. However, you should be aware that using the Lwa to harm others is something that will definitely come back to bite you on your sitter. To be clear, there's nothing sweet and cuddly about Ogou, but you can be sure he's protective, loyal, and nurturing in his own way. He can teach you how to stand up for what you hold true. He teaches courage and honor. There is no one more reliable and stronger than Ogou.

Lwa Correspondences

Note that with all Lwa, the specific information to serve them depends on the lineage you're with. Always defer to the elders when you need some clarity. Note that you can serve all the Lwa on Saturdays. However, you should not serve them on Sundays, anytime between Christmas and Epiphany, or during the Holy Week.

Papa Legba

Lwa Nation: Rada

Saints: Anthony of Padua, Lazarus, Peter

Days: Mondays or Thursdays

Colors: White/red, red, or purple/brown/gold.

Offerings: Rum, toasted corn or unsalted popcorn, a crutch or a cane, tobacco in a pipe, round straw bag, rice and beans, strong black coffee, cane syrup, cornbread.

Symbols: Cane, crossroads.

Concepts: Allowing communication with spirit, opening the road.

Damballah Wedo

Lwa Nation: Rada

Saints: Patrick (in south Haiti), Moses with the ten commandments (in north Haiti)

Day: Thursdays

Colors: White and deep green; pure white

Offerings: White foods like white bread, akasan, coconut, rice, milk, orgeat (almond syrup), Lotion Pompeia perfume, a white egg (uncooked) on a heap of white flour on a white plate.

Symbols: Earth, eggs, pythons, and the other constrictors.

Concepts: Peace, wealth, abundance, purity, creation, Earth.

Ayida Wedo

Lwa Nation: Rada

Saint: Our Lady of the Miraculous Medal (Miraculous Mother)

Day: Thursdays

Colors: Pastel rainbow colors, white.

Offerings: White foods like rice, akasan, coconut, white bread.

Symbols: Sky, snakes, rainbows.

Concepts: Peace, rainbows, purity, coolness.

Met Agwe Tawoyo

Lwa Nation: Rada

Saints: Archangel Raphael, Ulrich. (Both saints holding fish.)

Day: Thursdays.

Colors: Ocean colors, and gold and white and blue.

Offerings: Coffee with sugar and cream, champagne, melon, rice boiled in sweet milk, whole fish, cakes with white and blue icing, white goats, and rams.

Symbols: A ship or boat (Imamou), an admiral's hat, the ocean, flags, oars, conch shells, and all things related to boating, fishing, and the sea.

Concepts: The ocean and all its treasures.

La Siren

Lwa Nation: Rada.

Saints: Caridad del Cobre (Our Lady of Charity) or Diosa Del Mar (the Lady of the Sea).

Day: Thursdays.

Colors: Ocean colors, white, gold and silver, light blue.

Offerings: Perfume, champagne, a comb and mirror, pearls or seashells, rice boiled in sweet milk, silver jewelry or coins, whole fish, and cakes with white and blue icing,

Symbols: Dolphin, whale, mermaid.

Concepts: Water, wealth, nurturing, beauty, fertility, abundance.

Ezili Freda

Lwa Nation: Rada

Saint: Our Lady of Sorrows (Mater Dolorosa)

Day: Thursdays

Colors: Gold, soft pink, white

Offerings: Perfume (particularly Lotion Pompeia), cosmetics, mirrors, luxury items, fine jewelry, fancy cookies, fine candies, cakes with pink or white frosting, fine champagne, whole fish baked with no hot spices, flowers (especially pink or red roses)

Symbols: Jewelry, gold, hearts

Concepts: Femininity, desire, love

Chapter 5: The Violent Ones — Petwo Lwa

The Petwo Lwa are fierce, so you need to be careful while approaching them. Also called the Pedro Lwa, or Petro Lwa, or Dompete, sometimes people think of them as evil and assume the Rada Lwa are good, but this is very misleading. You can use the Rada Lwa to work evil magic and the Petwo Lwa to work good things. The thing about the latter, though, is that they work with more force. They don't know the meaning of the word "easygoing," unlike the Rada lwa. They are the fire to the Rada Lwa's ice. It's actually much better not to work with them if you don't have experience. Even experienced Vodouisants recommend not working with these Lwa.

Most of these Lwa are patrons of the Sanpwel, Zobop, and other secret societies. They have great power, and with that come great demands. If you don't greet them the right way, they're quick to get angry. If someone approaches them without respecting the correct ceremonies, then they're going to get in hot water. Should you decide to become an initiate of one of their societies, you'll get passwords and introductions you must use to greet the Lwa and work with them.

Ezili Danto

Also called Danto, her reputation is a mixed bag. Some see only her anger, sharp dagger, and scarred face, so they call her an evil spirit. The truth is she is a benevolent and loving mother, unafraid to empower her children with the strength to overcome all problems. As fierce a warrior as she is, she's also a loyal protector who will work hard and fast for those devoted to her.

Her colors are red and green or red and blue. Her altars are usually dressed in red cloth. She wears a dress of blue denim, like a peasant Haitian woman. She's one of the most important Lwa of the Petwo aspect. While her sister Freda is gentle and soft, Danto is strong. In the face of harsh truth, Freda weeps. Danto responds by throwing a shuddering, inarticulate tantrum with fists clenching and teeth grinding, stuttering, "Ke! Ke! Ke!" over and over, with the veins popping out on her head and neck. It's a hard sight to forget.

On her altar, you'll find a dagger with a sharp blade, a red headscarf, and a black doll. The doll wears blue-and-red calico or denim and holds a much smaller doll, too. On the doll's cheek are scratches that mirror Danto's scars. Griot is her best meal, and a black pig is her sacrificial animal. On her altar, you'll find a brand of cigarettes called Comme il Fauts. You can also use any unfiltered cigarettes. She also loves Florida water. Treat her respectfully and kindly, and she'll help you triumph in all your affairs and keep you safe. She cares for your children and brings opportunities to get rich. The wonderful thing about her is that she isn't fussy about gifts as long as you offer them to her with a sincere heart.

Kalfou

This Lwa is connected to the cemetery, death, and destruction. Go to Kalfou, the Lwa who shows up as a mighty warrior when you want to ignore the rules. Never approach him disrespectfully or carelessly. You need a proper introduction to interact with him. He's not evil, but he's aggressive and hot-tempered. It's better to ask him to stay away than to come to you. Still, if you're dealing with a lot of interpersonal issues, you can meet him at the crossroads with an offering for him to let you be. He is the one who empowers evildoers and sorcerers, so offering him something is a way to beg him to shut down their power supply.

You'll need a little bag of red flannel. Put three coins in it, as well as dirt from a courtroom, jail, or hospital. Add red cayenne pepper to the bag (you only need a pinch). By midnight, head out to a crossroads. It helps to have a holy symbol on you, like a star of David, pentagram, crucifix, or anything else that resonates with you and makes you feel protected.

At the crossroads, give Kalfou this speech: "Kalfou, please take your spirits away. Let them leave me be. Please shut your gates, that none will be able to send your mighty spirits to attack me. I've brought you this gift, so you can leave me be." Turn around, backing the crossroads, then toss the bag over your shoulder and off the road. Then head back home, and whatever you do, never look back. Throwing the bag away means your problems are gone as well. Also, make sure you head home through a different path than the way you got there. When you're home, cleanse yourself and your space.

Bossou

There is more than one Bossou, who is the bull Lwa. Bossou Twa Kon is the three-horned one. Kadja Bossou is part of the older root versions of this Lwa; Djobolo Bossou is known as Bossou the Devil, but it's unclear why, as he's not one of the evil ones. (Maybe because of his horns...?).

While Bossou may be venerated in his Rada aspect, this Lwa is seen as Petwo because his possessions are very violent. Those possessed by this Lwa begin to be tossed around violently as if being attacked by a raging ox. Some will butt their heads hard on hard surfaces like the Poteau Mitan. Bossou can also cause them to dance through fire or run on the ground set on fire.

Bossou is the Lwa that can help you out with major problems. If you're dealing with long-term unemployment, a stubborn issue that has refused to be fixed, call on Bossou and tell him what you're going through. Ask him to kindly bulldoze through all the troubles that stand in your way. You can promise him some barbecued chicken or roast beef for dinner. When you ask, you have to wait for him to act. Rest assured that you'll get an answer, especially if you honor him. You can also ask him to protect you and yours and offer him spicy food in appreciation.

Simbi

This Lwa is in charge of the brackish water you find in salt swamps. He's like the water snake, slender and fast. Typically, this spirit would rather remain on the periphery of ceremonies, as they're not entirely big on commotions. This is why mambos and houngans do what they can, to encourage them to enter the peristil. When the spirit does show up, it does so with force. Being possessed by Simbi can be a violent affair.

A shy spirit, Simbi will ignore anyone they don't like. Even if he likes you, it can be rather tricky to convince him to work with you. If you don't have this spirit, you may call on him forever, which would be pointless. This is why you should begin by leaving him little offerings in his favorite spots. Set some lemon drops on a little china plate and leave them by a well or stream. You could leave a cup of black coffee beneath the shade of a tree, saying, "I made this for you, Simbi. You can have it when you're ready." You can also offer him a little bottle of rum, putting it in or next to a salt swamp.

When you've made your offering, you need to write down your dreams. If you notice your dreams have water snakes in them, or someone comes and introduces themselves to you as Simbi, then he has acknowledged you. You've made each other's acquaintance. Note that Simbi may have very little to tell you initially, so these dreams may be short and sweet. Just write them down, continue to offer him things, and speak with him. Don't ask him to give you anything initially; rather, focus on getting to know one another. When he knows he can trust you, you'll have a powerful friend by your side. Without having trust in you, he won't do anything.

He's not a particularly demanding spirit and is very happy to offer you his service and protection for paying him attention now and then. You can light a candle in his honor on November 30 and offer him little things to make him happy. You can offer him things whenever you feel inspired to. If he shows up in a dream and asks you for something, or you get the sense that he'd like you to do something for him, then you should do as asked. If you want to be unnoticed or unseen, he can help you out. All you need to say is "Simbi, hide me," either aloud or under your breath.

Gran Bwa

Gran Bwa is friendlier than Petwo Lwa. His colors are green and red, and you can use scarves in those colors to set up an altar for him. He can be rather noisy when he arrives, throwing his horse with force in the early stage of possession. Still, he's usually in a pleasant mood. He will offer his protection and wisdom to the sosyete when approached with reverence and respect. He is syncretized with Saint Sebastian.

Gran Bwa lives in the forest, which means he finds it easy to feed himself, but Vodouisants still make a point of providing meals for him as a matter of courtesy. You can offer him cornmeal made with honey or beans and rice. Serve these on a plate, or even better, banana leaves. You may also make donations in his honor to charities interested in preserving the forests.

Igbo

Igbo or Ibo is part of the nations honored in Petwo. These people are not open to being bullied. They are proud, strong, and demanding. Gran Ibo is Ibos' grandmother, and Ibo Lele is one of the most popular and powerful Ibo spirits. These spirits offer different services depending on the houses, where they may or may not be served. Even when Ibo spirits aren't honored, you'll often find ceremonies with a clear Ibo influence.

When a member of the house dies, the sosyete performs the desounin rite, where the Lwa and the departed soul are separated. The soul moves on to heaven, while the spirits they had would pass on to someone else. Following this, the deceased is "taken out of the water" during *retire nan mo dio.* This ceremony involves invoking the dead person's spirit from the waters of the ancestors to install them in a special clay pot known as a *govi.* The spirit now lives in that pot and looks after the temple. It can also offer its counsel and advice, and sometimes you can hear it speak in hauntingly deep tones. These two ceremonies are rooted in Ibo ancestral service.

The Ibos believe those on earth are guarded and guided by those who have passed on; this explains why they honor their ancestors. In exchange, they receive their ancestors' assistance and protection. In native Igbo land, the dead communicate with the living through the *udu,* a clay drum that's fashioned after a water vessel with a hole in the side. Just as present-day Vodouisants do, the Ibos turn to their ancestors to keep them safe from evil forces. Also, like Vodouisants, most of them have traditional practices they follow alongside being practicing Catholics and Protestants. The Ibos honor those who have passed on and their personal Chi, using offerings, prayers, sacrifices, and reverence. Like the Haitians, they don't call on Chi-Ukwu (the Ultimate Creator) willy-nilly but seek out the assistance of their ancestors and personal Chi.

Most Africans brought to America during the slave trade were Ibos, so you might have some Ibo in your blood if you're an African American. It makes sense to honor your ancestors with some yam stew or okra soup (okra cooked in palm oil) along with pounded yams. Honoring them this way earns you their protection. Even if you're not Ibo, you can make offerings to atone for those you've wronged who are no more or those you owe ancestral debts. A good offering is a bowl full of clean water they can drink, kola nut, or palm wine. Set their meals on a red cloth and light a white candle for them. The best thing you can seek the Ibo spirits out for is courage and dignity. The Ibos are a proud people, and even during the slave trade, they would rather kill themselves than submit to their white masters.

Djabs

Djabs aren't Catholic or African spirits, and they're neither angels nor ancestors. You can call on these strong spirits to harm or heal. Rather tough to control and very unpredictable, these powerful guards work hard. As Vodou is a practical way of life, the Vodouisant prefers to work with Lwa for more practical life issues. Spirits less known to people will work faster and more effectively than the popular ones. Think of it this way: The local policeman just around the corner will be more likely to catch a thief than the police chief who's back at the precinct behind his desk. In the same way, Djabs bring you what you want faster than the other Lwa, who are followed by many and have numerous petitions to handle. The Djabs are like independent contractors who don't have to report to anyone and only serve the people who serve them.

Some of these Lwa are associated with specific places. In Haiti, most caves serve as homes to Djabs. They can travel from these caves to wherever, but they head back when they're done with their work. People who work with these spirits often have to travel to those caves to make their sacrifices and offerings. Some of these Djabs are tied to specific houses, sosyetes, or families. They are passed down from one generation to the next along with the guidelines for their care. Vodouisants don't say much in public about their Djabs. They know some will accuse them of dealing with devils, and others will try to steal these spirits.

While the word *Djab* is from the French word *diable*, these creatures are not diabolical. There are just wild spirits, but wildness doesn't imply malevolence. Having said that, some of them are connected with devils and spirits. Some of the beings, thought of as demons, are summoned by mambos and houngans. Those who "work with both hands" or two-handed magicians will serve beings like Le Roi Lecife (King Lucifer). They work with forces of good while being willing to call on dark forces to get what they or their clients need. These dark beings are known for their rage, dishonesty, and ferocity. It's best not to approach the evil Djabs at all.

Maitre Carrefour

Maitre Carrefour is the Master and Guardian of the Crossroads, considered Eshu Elegbara's alter-ego, shadow side, mirror image, or nighttime counterpart. Eshu Elegbara is the same as Legba or Elegba; he is also a sun or solar spirit. Maitre Carrefour, on the other hand, belongs to the moon. Legba is a trickster who may be more playful in his antics. Maitre Carrefour's trickery is taken to the extreme. The crossroad is when you have to make a decision, so when you metaphorically arrive at one, the road you choose (or don't choose) can greatly impact the rest of your life. So, when dealing with crossroad spirits like Maitre Carrefour, you need to be careful. They're supposed to lead you the right way, but if Maitre Carrefour is in the mood for a nasty prank, he could send you off the wrong way.

Crossroads are a witch's favorite spot. Ghosts and spirits love to hang out there as well. They're all under the authority of this very tricky Lwa who walks those paths at night accompanied by evil spirits to whom he is both gatekeeper and master. He decides which spirits and ghosts can pass. At night, he unleashes these spirits to wreak havoc, but you can petition him to keep them out of your business. However, this should only be done when all other options have failed. He is very powerful and dangerous, so you should never summon him for petty matters and never get too comfortable with him either.

https://pixabay.com/photos/garden-grass-leaves-logs-path-1839335/

Generally speaking, you really don't want him to pay attention to you unless you have a very good reason. If you feel you must work with him, then you should reach out to a houngan or mambo to intercede with him on your behalf. This spirit is aggressive and doubly effective. Work done with his assistance will lead to rapid results, and this is why his devotees are ever loyal to him. Every demon is under his command.

Maitre Carrefour is also very quick to punish. He's not particularly patient or good-natured, so never make promises that you cannot deliver right away. This is surely not a spirit for beginner Vodouisants to work with. He thinks fast, is brilliant, and tricky to boot, so you should never assume you could outwit him. He's the one to petition to keep evil people, ghosts, and spirits far from you. He'll help you break curses, spells, and hexes. If anyone has set evil spirits or spells after you, he can help you deflect them and keep them from ever getting to you. He is lord of the night and darkness, after all, so he would know best how to shield you from evil attacks.

Maitre Carrefour is also called Met Kalfou or Kalfu, his animal is the black pig, and his color is black. His special numbers are 7 and 3. At midnight, he is the sun, but at midday, he is the moon. If you're going to set up an altar in his honor, keep it strictly his, for he doesn't like to share with other spirits. You can offer him rum set on fire, but please be very careful with this, so you don't hurt yourself or burn the place down. You should also generously spice his food with habanero powder, cayenne pepper, or hot sauce

Marinette

The start of the Haitian Revolution was at Bois Caiman at a Vodou ceremony where the mambo involved Ogun and Ezili Danto by sacrificing a black pig. It is believed that Marinette is a princess who was eventually deified as a Lwa. She continues to relate well with Ogun and Ezili Danto. Being a solitary Lwa, she is mysterious in all her ways and is part of the Bizango pantheon and the Petwo.

Her life was difficult, so she's bitter and would rather be alone because she was disappointed in life by many. The French colonial forces pursued her aggressively. On top of that, she never got to have any glory for her part in the Haitian Revolution. This was because the leader of the movement, Toussaint L'Ouverture, had declared the frontlines a no-go area for women. Even to this day, she's seen as an evil spirit. She is the spirit of frustration and rage but also of justice.

Marinette is controversial. Vodouisants say that she shouldn't be invoked because she is hostile and dangerous, and you should definitely not invoke her as a newcomer to Vodou. Also, the fact that she's a priestess means she knows right away if you're a novice or an adept, so please don't think you can deceive her. Never invoke her in the house or any building, as it's not a safe thing to do. Her rage is a wildfire that burns — *literally* burning buildings and their occupants. She's a Lwa invoked by secret sosyetes, sorcerers, and expert initiates to discipline those who do evil. She hates when people abuse power and works hard to set innocents free from oppression and bullying.

This Lwa is the matron of loups-garoux (French for werewolves). She's syncretized to the Anima Sola or Joan of Arc. She is also called Marinette Bwa-Cheche, meaning "Marinette of the Dry Arms." She is left-handed, representing her willingness to work for hire and carry out unethical requests. Her red eyes are a metaphor for her rage. She has aviary features, with feet and hands resembling claws, and her bird is a screech owl. Her element is fire, her attributes are stake and cross, and her colors are black and red.

Don Petro

Now, let's wrap up this chapter with none other than Don Petro, who founded the Petro or Petwo Vodou tradition. His full name was Jean-Philippe Pedro, a Vodouisant who led the Maroons. The word *Maroon* is from the word *Cimarron*, which means "wild one." That is what runaway slaves were called. They formed entire communities in remote places where they fiercely opposed colonial rulers and slavery by forming resistance movements.

In 1768, the Don created the Petro tradition. Sometimes, the ceremonies would get violent and terrifying to the colonials. The Petwo Lwas and faithful followers are fired up by defiance and never allow themselves to be patronized or condescended to. They're definitely not okay with being ordered about.

When Don Petro died, he became a Lwa, known as the tradition's ancestor and therefore the ancestor of his devotees. He is all about resisting the oppression from colonials and their lackeys on behalf of devotees. He and Ezili Dantor are the spiritual parents of all of the Petro pantheon. This could be interpreted literally. It could also point to them just being the couple in charge of this tradition, similar to how Ayizan and Loko lead the Rada Lwa.

Lwa Correspondences

Legba Petro

Lwa Nation: Petro

Saints: Jude (with a club or fire), Peter (with a rooster and keys)

Days: Mondays or Tuesdays

Colors: Red and black or red and white

Offerings: Keys, a crutch or walking stick, red headscarves (moushwa), beans and rice, mango, spicy bread, pipe tobacco, kleren

Sympos: Opening the crossroads to work magic

Concepts: Same as in Rada Legba, but more oriented to the Kongo and Petro spirits

Simbi-Dlo

Lwa Nation: Petro (Kongo)

Saints: Moses with the ten commandments (in south Haiti), John, the Baptist as a kid with a staff and a lamb

Day: Tuesdays

Color: Green and white

Offerings: Pictures of snakes, grilled pork, smooth stones or river rocks, kleren, clear, cool water.

Ezili Danto

Lwa Nation: Petro

Saints: Our lady of Czechostowa, Our Lady of Perpetual help (Mater Salvatoris), any "black Virgin" with a child in her hands

Days: Tuesdays

Colors: Gold and royal blue, or red and royal blue

Offerings: Pipe tobacco, kleren, griot, spicy grilled pork, pineapple, pork rinds (chicharrones), papaya, mango, creme de cacao liqueur, bright flowers, coffee with rum in it or strong black coffee, baby dolls with dark skin and dolls in general.

Symbols: The Madonna and Child, machetes and daggers, a dagger pierced through a heart.

Concepts: The Haitian woman and her necessities for life, womanhood, motherhood.

Simbi-Andezo

Lwa Nation: Petro (Kongo)

Saints: Moses with the Ten Commandments (south Haiti), Andrew, John the Baptist baptizing Christ (north Haiti)

Day: Tuesdays

Colors: Red and teal or red and green

Offerings: Seawater, feathers, and ribbons, pictures of snakes, grilled pork, river rocks, kleren, clear and cool water

Symbols: Water, snakes

Concepts: The power to be in two worlds simultaneously, protection, magic, water, the spirit world.

Chapter 6: The Masters of Death — Guede Lwa

Some believe that the first Guede was pulled out of the waters of death by the first houngan, Papa Loko. Others say that Baron Samedi did that or that the Taino and Arawak people are the origin of the Guede. In contrast, some claim that these spirits are from an African tribe called the Gede-Vi, decimated during a war shortly before the slavers got there. Regardless of where they're from, these spirits are greatly loved all through Haiti. These clowns who have passed on are very protective, ready to help you, and ever so amusing.

When they first show up at a fet, they do the banda dance, keeping a straight back while their hips swivel, forming the figure eight. The banda rhythm is played along with this dance, and its peculiar percussion is meant to mimic sexual intercourse.

When the Guede show up on Earth, they wear sunglasses, so the light doesn't hurt their eyes. They might sometimes remove one lens to see their food, wear their glasses the wrong way, or put on many pairs at once. They also apply powder on their face to mimic the pallor of death.

These Lwa are all about fertility and death. Among them are Guede Linto, Guede Doubye, Guede Nibo, Guede Loraj, and Guede Ti Malis. When they're doing the banda, they'll rub a mix of 21 goat or habanero peppers and raw rum or clairin all over themselves and may sometimes drink the mixture as well.

The Guede is also known as "mysteries and invisible." The word Guede itself translates to "the sacred dead." The Festival of the Ancestors is a celebration that honors the Lord of the dead. It takes place on November 2, which is also "All Souls' Day." At this festival, you can repay these Lwa for all they've done for you throughout the year. You can't afford to skip the fet. Otherwise, they will punish you for it. These beings are remarkable at healing, predicting the future, and protecting all who belong to them. Devotees put on mourning outfits to celebrate. When they're possessed, they might expose other followers' secrets, which can lead to confusion.

These Lwa are contacted by sorcerers who do magic with dead bodies. Be aware that you can't excavate bodies or invoke the spirits of those who are no more without getting the green light from the cemetery landlords. The Guede spirits can help sorcerers with their divination and meditation. They scoff in the face of sanctimony, love obscenities, ribaldry, and of course, sex. When infertility issues plague you, you can call on them for help.

A Peculiar Group of Lwa

The Guede is an interesting family of Lwa who doesn't care about being prim and proper. First of all, their drink of choice is Piman, which is raw rum with 21 peppers soaked in it. Those who pretend to be possessed by these spirits will inevitably burn their mouths badly by drinking Piman. The Guede can also show you that possession is genuine by washing their face with this mix. They'll even pour them in their eyes and wash their genitals with it, acting like it's nothing but water.

This group is known for being vulgar and using foul language, slang, and every offensive word they can. They also love to talk about sex and get a kick out of embarrassing others by leaking their secrets. They'll grind on people and talk about every sexual body part all day.

Many houngans and mambos serve a Gede on their clients' behalf. The spirit can offer more information to help them fix problems, offering truth and clarity. If they consider you snobby, they will embarrass you, so come to them with respect, if you must come to them at all. They have a great sense of humor and are full of mischief.

The Guede Lwa is syncretized with Saint Gerard Majella, who has a cross in hand and a skull on a table to the left. Saint Gerard also takes care of pregnant women and is connected with the Guede Lwa. The Guede can treat the womb of pregnant women or those who want to be pregnant but can't conceive.

Guede Linto

This Lwa is popular because he works miracles. Standing around 5 feet tall, this old man with dark skin wears glasses, an old-timey black hat, and a cane. His manners are impeccable, and he's rather docile — so much that many assume he's just a little boy.

Guede Linto loves teaching his devotees how to sing. He gifts things made from rum, Florida water, fire, and cigarettes. He cuts a bit of thread for each devotee and drops them in a special mix to create needles. Sometimes, he gives gold chains and rings as gifts and puts them into knots which he makes out of their scarves.

Linto is fiercely protective of children. He represents all lost children and the aborted, neglected, stillborn, and miscarried ones. He also cares for those who were abused to the point of death. He's the youngest Guede Lwa, so he causes his devotees to act childishly and walk like babies, just like they are learning how to use their legs. They can also cry and babble for food.

When he works, expect immediate and accurate solutions. He can spot trouble coming towards you half a year away and can either help you through it or show you how to stop it.

Papa Guede

The corpse of the first man ever to die is Papa Guede. He's short, dark, and wears a high hat. He loves to eat apples and smoke cheap cigars. He waits at the crossroads, ready to take souls who have passed on to the afterlife. He's Baron Samedi's counterpart as well. When a kid is dying, it's Papa Guede that everyone prays to because it's believed that he never takes anyone's life until it's their time to go. Only he can keep the little ones safe. His sense of humor is rather crass, but don't let that put you off. He can read everyone's mind and knows what's likely to happen in this world and the next.

He has many names, like Bawon Lakwa (meaning "Baron of the Cross," and so on. He is in charge of the Guede rites as well. His colors are white, black, and purple, and he can be represented with a coffin or a cross. If you need help with a legal problem or you want justice, reach out to the Baron.

Brave Guede

This is the watchman and guardian of the graveyard. He's the one who makes sure that the dead stay in, and the living stay out. He's also thought of as one of Nibo's aspects.

Guede Double

This Guede Lwa can offer you "second sight" or clairvoyance as a gift.

Guede Babaco

This is Papa Guede's brother. He's not as well-known as Papa but is a psychopomp like him. He plays a similar role to Papa Guede, but he doesn't have the abilities his brother does.

Guede L'Orage

This Guede will only show up when there is a storm. He is also called Guede L'Oraj.

Guede Nibo

A psychopomp, this Guede lwa is a go-between for the dead and the living. He was the first person ever to die as a result of violence. This is why he's the patron of all souls who died due to violent, unnatural causes, including accidents, disasters, and misadventure. He guards the graves of souls that passed on before their time, especially those whose actual resting place remains a mystery. Those he possesses can speak on behalf of the dead spirits whose bodies are missing or haven't been reclaimed from under the waters.

Guede Ti Malice

This Lwa is a trickster and the nemesis of Tonton Bouki. He is full of guile and very smart. He also works hard, but at the same time, he is very greedy, which makes it hard to drive a fair bargain with him.

Guede Massaka

This Guede helps Guede Nibo. He's androgynous, and you can recognize him by his white jacket, black shirt, and white headscarf. He carries a gris-gris bag with poison in it.

Guede Oussou

This Guede wears a mauve or black jacket with a white cross on the back, along with a mauve or black headscarf. *Oussou* means "tipsy." This is an apt name because he absolutely loves his white rum.

Baron Kriminel

This is the Baron of Criminals and the Guede's enforcer. He was the first murderer, with his victim likely being Nibo. This is why he is the master of those who hurt others with violence and people who are murderers.

The families of murdered and/or abused souls will pray to the Baron to get revenge. His possessed devotees have quite a ravenous appetite and will attack everyone until you offer them food. If the food takes too long or doesn't please them, they'll chew and bite anyone who is close – even themselves – until they feel sated. Baron Kriminel is syncretized with Saint Martin de Porres. He is offered a sacrifice of black roosters on the Guede feast day. The roosters need to be bound, dipped in strong spirit, and lit up to burn.

Maman Brigitte

Also known as Mother Bridget, she is Baron Samedi's wife, syncretized with Saint Brigit. She is associated with cemeteries, death, motherhood, and fertility. She usually wears very sexual outfits, exudes femininity, and is as dangerous as she is sensual. She's a powerful healer who will help her devotees in the afterlife if she can't cure or heal them. In particular, she's called upon to heal sexually transmitted diseases and conditions that cause infertility. She is also invoked to offer her divine judgment. When wickedness needs to be punished, she works swiftly and with no mercy. In a cemetery, the first woman buried has her grave marked with a unique cross that belongs to this Lwa.

Maman Brigitte protects fiercely. She keeps her loving, watchful eyes over all the women who ask for her help — especially those dealing with childbirth, unfaithful partners, or domestic violence.

This Lwa, unlike others, isn't from Africa but from Ireland. She has red hair and fair skin. Her devotees know the best thing to offer her is a rum infused with hot peppers. You can also offer her black roosters and candles. When she possesses her devotees, they'll rub the spicy, hot rum on their privates. Her veve sometimes is a black rooster on top of a cross and will sometimes include a heart.

She can be venerated on All Souls' Day or on February 2, Saint Brigid's feast day. The Vodouisants put out a scarf or some other piece of clothing overnight and ask her to imbue it with her healing power. This Lwa is tough and is very much at ease with allowing a stream of profanity to run out her mouth when she is enraged by those who have done wrong or displeased her.

The Ancestors

In Haitian culture, these are very crucial spirits. The countryside has many family graveyards. These families died in very complicated ways, and their tombs are elaborate and resemble little houses above ground with stairs that lead to the underground where the crypt is. The wealthier families will have living rooms in their tombs, and all over the grave you'll find pictures of the ones who have gone. It matters that when you're in a family compound, you pay your respects at the tomb, and then they may welcome you.

The Baron leads the ancestors, guiding them in all matters, as he is the head of the cemetery. You can reach out to the ancestors for help in all matters and seek their wise counsel.

Lwa Correspondences

Baron Samedi

Lwa Nation: Gede

Saints: Expedite, Gabriel

Day: Fridays

Colors: White, purple, black

Offerings: Stale bread, Piman, strong black coffee, cigarettes, very spicy food, sunglasses, a top hat, a phallic cane (painted with white and black stripes)

Symbols: Skulls, cemetery crosses, top hat, bones, coffins, shovels, sunglasses, tools for digging graves

Concepts: Fertility and life, the dead and death, children as the future, sexual regeneration

Manman Brijit

Lwa Nation: Gede

Saints: Rita (in some parts), Rosalia

Day: Fridays

Colors: Purple, black, white

Offerings: Mirrors, dried flowers, sunglasses, a bonnet or hat, cigarettes, very spicy food, strong black coffee, stale bread, Piman

Symbols: Trees, bones, coffins, skulls, cemetery crosses

Concepts: Fertility and life, the dead and death, children as the future, sexual regeneration, protection of businesses as a means of sustaining life

Brav Gede (Along with the Rest of the Gede)

Lwa Nation: Gede

Saints: Gerard Majella, and now and then, Martin de Porres

Day: Fridays

Colors: White, purple, black

Offerings: Stale bread, Piman, strong black coffee, cigarettes, very spicy food, sunglasses, a top hat, a phallic cane (painted with white and black stripes)

Symbols: Skulls, cemetery crosses, top hat, bones, coffins, shovels, sunglasses, tools for digging graves

Concepts: Fertility and life, the dead and death, children as the future, sexual regeneration.

Chapter 7: Vodou Altars and Dolls

Haitian Vodou is usually practiced in an ounfo, but you have the option of setting up an altar at home. This chapter will show you everything you need to know about creating a proper altar and the importance of dolls.

About Your Altar...

https://unsplash.com/photos/black-wooden-altar-YuGIIMEhyEY

There are many ways by which you can serve the Lwa using your altar, and you don't have to break the bank if you can't afford to or don't want to. The Lwa simply asks for sincerity in your service and nothing more. You can use the things around your home to set up your altar. Newcomers to Vodou don't realize that they already have enough stuff in their homes to make great offerings to the Lwa. For instance, spoons, knives, and forks can work as offerings. You could spare a bit of food, offer some aspirin and a band-aid to Maman Brigitte, or give Gran Bwa some nice leaves. You could offer the Baron some dirt on a plate, give Ogou matches, lighters, and knives, or give Agwe and La Sirene seashells if you have those lying around. Legba's pretty cool with old keys as well.

The important thing to do is research the Lwa you're serving and find out what they want, then place a representation of that thing on the altar. You can also put pictures that are connected to them. You don't have to take the pictures yourself. Just print them off the internet.

If you don't have enough money, you can head to the dollar store and find many items which you can use for your altar for less than a dollar. The Lwa don't care if you got a Vodou set from Gucci or somewhere else. The most important thing is your intention and the respect you give while serving. If all you have is a glass of water, they're good with that as well. You need to understand that Vodou isn't about money but about spirit, heart, mind, love, respect, and sincerity. If you feel drawn to worship these Lwa, don't concern yourself too much about whether you have the means or not. There's nothing wrong with humble means.

Altars have to be fed and awakened. They'll wax and wane in power. They are living, breathing things with their stories to tell, connecting the divine with humanity. They show the state of being, who you are individually and within the context of society. They can be beneath your skin, in a bottle, or in your attic. You can set them wherever you want — even at a grave.

Before You Set Up Your Home Altar

If you decide to serve the Lwa, you might find it useful to have a special place to offer your service. Your altar can be at home so that it's easy for you to be consistent in your practice. It should be at a place where you can present your gifts to the spirits, make requests, and just connect with the Lwa.

Before you set up your altar, you need to reach out to mambo or houngan so they can let you know the Lwa that chooses you. When it comes to Vodou, you don't get to pick your spirits. They pick you. So, you must serve the ones who choose you. They want your service and would happily reward you for it. So please approach a mambo or houngan for a reading.

A good reason to reach out to a priestess or priest before you create your altar is to have all possible questions answered. You need to know as much as you can about the Lwa who choose to walk with you so that you can serve them the right way. You need to know about their correspondences and all that they require from you.

Damballah Wedo might want you to put out an egg for him on a bed of sugar so that your life can be sweet. Ezili Danto might want you to bring a knife so she can work with you. These are the things you learn from a Vodou priest or priestess. They can teach you about the saints, colors, and items connected to the Lwa. This information changes from house to house, so you should stick with just one source to avoid being overwhelmed or confused. It's best if you're already part of a house and have spiritual parents guiding you, as these parents can teach you all about the Lwas of that house.

When you first pick a spot for your home altar, you have to baptize it. It's even better if a mambo or houngan can help you with this process, making it more attractive to your Lwa. If you can't get them to help, here's what you need to do:

1. Dust the table and clean it thoroughly.

2. Mix Florida water, Holy Water, and basil together.

3. Wash down the surface of your altar with this mixture. As you do, say to the table, "I cleanse you in the name of the Father, the Son, and the Holy Spirit, that only the spirits that desire my good and bring me good things gather here. Let all who seek to bring me down find this place inhabitable."

4. Let the surface air dry, and then you can construct your altar.

You'll have to set up the altar precisely for the Lwa that chooses you. So, it would be wise to talk to mambo or houngan about which spirits are fine being set next to each other.

Another thing to be clear about is that even if several Lwa choose you, you don't have to have them all on your table simultaneously. You can start with one spirit. Begin by pouring them some water, and take time getting to know them. When you sense that your relationship with them is ready to go, you can add another Lwa to your sacred space.

You don't have to get chromoliths or statues before you begin setting up your altar. It's a living thing that continues to evolve. Your altar could never be finished because it's always going to be in a state of progress. So, if you find there's something you'd like to set on it, but you don't have it right now, you can put it on your altar later. It's better to start with the stuff you do have and can easily acquire, then work your way from there over time. If all you own are a bottle of alcohol and some prayer cards, that's also fine. Set those on the altar, and when you can afford to get one, you can put a chromolith or a statue on it.

Another Way to Set Up an Ogantwa

The home altar is also called *ogantwa.* It could be a table or cabinet, a shelf, or some furniture that has divided sections. Here's another way to set it up:

1. Cover your ogantwa with white cloth made of satin, cotton, or any other spotless and smooth fabric.

2. Behind the ogantwa, place the picture of Saint Claire or Klemezin Klermey, who brings illumination and clarity. You can set other images as well, or just leave Saint Claires' alone.

3. In front of Saint Claire and on the ogantwa should be a Santissima or a standing crucifix. If you prefer, you can just hang a crucifix above Saint Claire on the wall.

4. On one side of your ogantwa, set a white candle.

5. Set a red candle on the other side. You could use a multicolored one instead.

https://unsplash.com/photos/shallow-focus-photo-of-four-red-lighted-candles-c72eCrOstC4

6. Put Florida water, Pompeii, fresh flowers, frankincense, and Holy Water on the altar. If you don't have Florida water, Rev d'Or is fine.

7. Set a bowl or glass of fresh water on the altar.

8. If you want, set a bell or kwakwa rattle on the ogantwa. You'll use this to call your spirits.

9. Beneath your altar, keep your ritual items like a small brazier or censer, a glass bowl, taper candles, holy olive oil, and other things of the sort.

10. Now, it's time to baptize the ogantwa before you use it. To do so, burn frankincense in your brazier or censer.

11. As the frankincense burns, say the Lord's prayer thrice and Hail Mary Seven times. You can learn the prayers by heart before making your altar. They'll come right after these instructions.

12. Sprinkle Holy water on your Ogantwa as you say, "I baptize you in the name of the Father, the Son, and the Holy Spirit. I consecrate you for good deeds and good spirits only. Amen."

The Lord's Prayer

Our Father, who art in heaven,

hallowed be thy name; thy kingdom come;

thy will be done on earth as it is in heaven.

Give us this day our daily bread;

and forgive us our trespasses

as we forgive those who trespass against us;

and lead us not into temptation,

but deliver us from evil. Amen.

Hail Mary

Hail Mary, full of grace.

The Lord is with thee.

Blessed art though amongst women;

and blessed is the fruit of thy womb, Jesus Christ.

Holy Mary, mother of God,

pray for us sinners, now and at the hour of our death.

Setting Up Your Home Altar

1. When you've chosen your table and cleansed and blessed it, use a white cloth to cover it. The white cloth should go all the way down to the ground. You can let it go halfway down if you're setting the Guede beneath the table.

2. One half of your table will be for the Rada Lwa, while the other will be for the Petro lwa. Use a lovely white cloth for the Rada on the right-hand side. On the left, use a cloth that's an intense and bright shade of red to represent the Petro Lwa.

3. Set pictures or chromoliths of the Lwa you're serving to the wall right behind your altar. Before choosing the pictures, you should get a proper reading from a mambo or hougan to determine which spirits are with you first.

4. Feel free to add any figures or statues you have to represent your spirits. Not all Lwa will need a statue. For Ezili Danto, a little baby doll dressed in earrings and necklaces will do. For Damballah Wedo, you can have a white serpent statue and/or a Saint Patrick statue; for the Marassa, you can set small identical dolls. Ti Jean Dantor would be fine with a statue of the baby Saint John the Baptist.

5. Next, set the spirits' favorite food, drinks, and other items they love.

Tips on Making Vodou Altars

You don't have to be a mambo or hougan yourself to create your altar. You can set these altars up for public or private use. The important thing to remember when creating yours is that you must do so with respect and sincerity. Vodou is a very tolerant religion in which it rarely excludes anything. You can see this from the fact that it's an amalgamation of various African beliefs.

Whether you set up your altar in a cupboard, on a table, or a shelf, there are certain things you should always keep in mind:

- Keep beautiful things, talismans, Vodou dolls, flowers, statues, stones, or roots on your altar. These things should mean something to you or inspire you.

- You can put anointing oils, perfumes, incense, and candles on the altar as well. It's even better when these things are specifically what your Lwa likes.

- You have to put some water on the altar to represent coolness and clarity in your life. Make sure to keep the water fresh by changing it often.

- You can set up your altar in honor of the dead or living or anyone you draw inspiration from. You should set their pictures on the altar as well.

- You can make your altar as complex or simple, plain, or beautiful as you'd like.

- Make a point of heading to your altar first thing in the morning and last thing at night to start and end the day with your Lwa.

- Meditate at this altar each day, feeding and filling your mind with the manifestation of your desires and positive changes you seek on behalf of yourself, your family, or others.

Voodoo Dolls

Image by Bill Couch
https://www.flickr.com/photos/wcouch/3464210637

Contrary to popular opinion, dolls are used in honor of the Lwa and not for torturing people as popular media would have you believe. If you ever thought about making your own doll, you're in luck. You don't need anything fancy and can easily work with the natural materials lying around your home.

Dolls matter in Vodou because they serve as a communication channel between you and the Lwa. They can also help you reach your target, no matter where they may be. You can make them out of cotton, silk, wood, or any other material, but here's a list of the basic things you need:

- Hemp rope
- Two sticks
- Fabric glue
- White and black embroidery thread or waxed nylon thread

- Pins and needles
- Patterns
- Fine leather
- Scraps of cloth, feathers, buttons, and other knick-knacks to dress the doll
- Strat, herbs, or any other stuffing material
- Paper
- Scissors
- Cardboard

The doll is supposed to represent a person, so you might find it best to dress it up by adding a personal touch. You can use items of clothing, hair, makeup, and so on.

Making Your Vodou Doll

1. With the two sticks, create a cross by placing the shorter one perpendicular to the long one.

2. With the thread, knot both sticks. Work with an X-shape so that you have a cross when you're done.

3. The lower part of the long pole is the body, while the upper part is the head. Both sides of the short pole are the arms.

4. With the stuffing, wrap the poles. It's best to begin at the middle, then work your way up and around the head, then one arm after the other, before finally making it to the bottom part.

5. Use pieces of cloth to cover the doll. To keep all items on the Vodou doll, you can use glue to hold the cloth in place and sew what you must. Please keep a bit of filler exposed on the arms' ends, on the bottom, and head.

6. On the doll's head, fix some beads to form the mouth and eyes.

7. Now, dress this doll with your target's personal effects. Putting a piece of their hair will give even more power to the doll.

8. When you're done, consecrate it and then use holy water to baptize it.

How Vodou Dolls Work

Dolls work by way of sympathetic magic. Sympathetic magic is the magic of correspondence. You use an item to represent an idea or a person or whatever else you want. When you create a doll to stand for someone and dress it up with their personal effects, you've effectively created a connection between that person and the doll. So, when you bless or harm the doll, the target is affected. When you follow the steps for creating a doll correctly and make sure you cast your spells the right way, your requests will be granted in no time. They will happen with no regard for distance, especially since you're working with Lwa's help.

Properly Disposing of a Doll

Say you have a negative doll you want to get rid of. Burning it isn't a good idea, as you might be setting fire to the target you've linked it to. To get rid of it, wrap it in a clean, white cloth and sprinkle it with sea salt. Take it out to the woods or the river, where you can call on the spirits to transmute the doll's energy from negative to positive or unlink the doll from the target. You can leave the doll in the woods or toss it into a flowing river when you've done this. Whichever method you choose, make sure you walk away without looking back. When you get home, you can cleanse yourself spiritually in a sea salt bath.

Chapter 8: Vodou in Santeria and Candomble

The Difference between Hoodoo, Vodou, and Santeria

Far too often, Santeria is mixed up with other African religious and magical systems. The media refers to Santeria Lucumi or Lukumi practices as Vodou. Everything is just lumped together as the same thing, only to be mocked or sensationalized and maligned with cultural misinformation. The confusion between Hoodoo and Voodoo adds more fuel to the fire of confusion about what Santeria actually is. So, we're going to clear all of that up in this chapter.

Vodou and Santeria

Image by Adam Cohn
https://www.flickr.com/photos/adamcohn/48863506097

Also called "Lukumi's Rule," Santeria means "way of the saints" or "honor of the saints." Voodoo means "moral fiber." These are both African traditional religions, but that doesn't make them the same.

First of all, Vodou, or Voodoo, has two main branches. You have the Louisiana Vodou (New Orleans) and Haitian Vodou. It's a religion of the African diaspora, an amalgamation of different religious practices of various tribes, some of which were rivals. However, they had come to depend on each other during the dark days of slavery. Among these tribes are the Yoruba, Fon, Congo, and Taino. They brought their practices together to help them survive and formed a regleman or ritual order meant to honor every tribe's spirits in worship. French Catholicism also influenced their practices in the process of syncretism.

You already know the spirits are classed as Rada, Petwo, or Gede. The Rada Lwa are the orishas and Vudu of the Yoruba and Fon people, respectively. The Petwo Lwa are from the Congo's fiery spirits and those of the modern-Haitian and Taino people. Veves are cornmeal drawings, very ornate, and laid out on tables or on the ground. They are used for summoning the Lwa in Vodou, but this isn't something Santeria involves. Haitian Vodou has an initiated priesthood, but you don't have to be an initiate to practice this religion. In fact, many Vodouisants aren't initiated. The gris-gris and magical wanga feature prominently in Vodou magic. Kreyol is the liturgical language of this religion, being the Haitian French local dialect.

Louisiana Vodou is very different from Haitian Vodou, as it's a potpourri of the magical and religious practices from the south of the United States. The religion does include some of the Lwa from Haitian Vodou. There's a predominance of Catholic saints and influences from southern folk magic such as mojo bags, gris-gris, and wanga. This religion has no regleman, and it encourages self-made queens of Vodou. It's strongly tied with spiritualism and has many techniques inspired by southern folk magic, which you shouldn't confuse with Hoodoo. Louisiana Vodou also uses Veves, and its liturgical language is English mixed with a touch of French Creole.

Santeria developed in Cuba and is rooted in the Yoruba religious traditions that you can find in present-day Nigeria. Those who follow this path worship the Orishas, who are the Yoruba people's demigods. You will find a touch of Spanish Catholicism, especially as an outsider. Still, when you're initiated, that falls to the side. The Catholic elements in this religion are similar to those in Espiritismo, a religion deeply connected with Santeria.

Santeria involves initiation rites, is secretive, and has very strict rules. Most participants are initiates. Santeria doesn't work with veves or drawing to invoke the Orisha as is done in Vodou. Sure, some rituals use paintings called *osun*, but these do not resemble veves at all. Here, the liturgical language is Lukumi, a Yoruba dialect from the 1800s, mixed with some Cuban Spanish elements.

The magical workings and religious practices of these traditions may all seem alike. However, they are anything but the same. The Santeria initiate has no right to partake in Vodou ceremonies, the same way a Vodouisant doesn't have permission to be part of a Santeria ceremony. These two religions are very different when it comes to language, songs, prayers, and rituals. The only thing they all share in common is animal sacrifice and the use of magic and spells as part of the practice.

The main tenet of Santeria is to always be in a place of blessings or *Ire,* and the way to do this is to follow the wise words of the elders, egun, and orishas. The believers are particular about helping others, doing their best to lift their fellow humans out of sickness and poverty and into health, blessings, longevity, and prosperity. They respect everyone around them, as well as mother nature. They work with magic as a form of defense against those who would seek to harm them.

Santeria is focused on fostering and bettering relationships between humans and the divine, powerful spirits known as the Orishas. They are manifestations of God or *Olodumare.* You can see how this is similar to Haitian Vodou beliefs. The followers of Santeria believe that these spirits can help them in life when they correctly perform the appropriate rites. This will allow them to unlock the true destiny set for them by God before they were even born. For the Orishas to continue their service, they need to be worshipped.

Santeria also has Roman Catholic influences. For instance, Shango is the embodiment of strength and justice and is syncretized with Saint Barbara. This Orisha is connected to fire and lightning. Ochun is the Yoruba goddess of the river, syncretized with Our Lady of Charity. She is associated with matters of love, money, the color yellow, water, and sweets. Babalu Aye is syncretized with Saint Lazarus and connected to those who are sick.

The rituals of this religion allow humans to connect with the Orishas through drumming, dancing, eating, and speaking with the divine beings. There are buildings dedicated to the way of the saints. The followers participate in rituals in halls they rent out or in private homes fitted with altars to allow proper worship. During these rituals, Orishas can connect with the faithful.

The Bembe ritual is one of the most important rituals in Santeria, where the Orisha are invited to join the devoted community by singing, dancing, and drumming. During these rituals, the Orisha may take over the head of a devotee (or "seize the head," or "mount" them, as it's described). Once mounted, the devotee begins to dance spectacularly. They also pass on important messages from the world of spirit to the humans in attendance.

Animals are sacrificed as food for the participants of the ritual and the priest. Followers offer the sacrificed animals as food to the Orisha to build a better bond with the spirit and grow even closer to them. This practice helps devotees become more aware that they carry the Orisha within them wherever they go. It is said that the Orishas need this food, else they'll die if not fed. The Orishas also feed on praise and worship. Devotees can offer sacrifices for all sorts of things like death, marriage, birth, and promotion. Sometimes they offer sacrifices for healing, too.

However, when it's a death or healing rite, the food from the animal will not be eaten. This is because the sickness moves into the dead animal, so eating it would cause you to take on the illness or invite death into your life. When devotees eat the animal, they commune with the Orisha. The latter only takes the animal's blood while the devotees feast on the cooked meat. Most commonly sacrificed animals are chickens, doves, pigeons, ducks, goats, guinea pigs, turtles, and sheep. According to the Supreme Court of the United States of America, it is constitutional for Santeria devotees to kill these animals for their religious purposes.

Organization in Santeria

There's no central body that organizes the practice of Santeria. The main unit of the Santeria community is a house, known as an *ile* (the Yoruba word for house) or casa (the Spanish word for house). This house belongs to a senior Santeria priest who leads an extended family. This priest is more often a female than a male and is the head of the house and the family. You can think of them as a godmother or godfather to brothers and sisters in spirit.

The devotees understand that the main purpose of the ile is to honor the Orisha and gain assistance and guidance from them in every aspect of life. The Orishas are generous in giving their children divine wisdom and sharing their spiritual experiences, marked by the upward progression through the ile's hierarchy. The Ile carves out a path to attain spiritual heights.

The family in an ile connects with one another the same way extended family members who are biologically related would do. There's also a hierarchy loosely based on the stages of spiritual attainment that the members have reached. The ile may be small or large, but they're all independent. Now and then, several iles come together for special rites.

Membership is very important in Santeria, and everyone must be part of the ile. People called to work with the Orisha often do so as an adult, having had the call from one of these beings. For some, they were faced with a life-threatening situation that forced them to seek out the Orisha for help, and that was how their journey began. One of the ways the Orisha call people is through illness, to awaken the new devotee and make them aware of their true purpose of life: Service to the divine. Devotees enter a pact with the Orisha, understanding that the spirit has the power to take their lives and that they should show deep appreciation for being cured of their illness. When you're initiated into Santeria, it's a solemn affair; one that changes your life and connects you to your Orisha and a whole new family.

The Priesthood in Santeria

The priesthood has women and men, and training and initiation are necessary before you can be a part of it. The priest could be an *iyalorisha* (which means "Wife or Mother in the Spirit") or a *babalorisha* (meaning "Father in the spirit"). Those are Yoruba words. In Spanish, they're called the *santero* (priest) or *santera* (priestess). Being a part of the priesthood doesn't mean you can't do anything else, as it's not a full-time job. When you've "made the saint" as a priest, it means you've been "reborn in the spirit," and therefore, you are committed in service to a certain Orisha. Priests have unique powers as they've been "entered" by spirit. Some would say that's demonic possession, but that's not the case. Remember, demons and Satan are ideas that aren't part of the Santeria religion.

Divination

Divination is very much a part of Santeria. It's the power to predict the future and a mediation process between Orun (heaven) and Aiye (earth), where one can get brilliant guidance and counsel at important transitional phases of life. Divination can be done using a split coconut, gleaning meaning from how shells fall or casting palm nuts. Santeria involves Ifa, a system of divination that belongs to the Yoruba people. This form of divination is only performed by the *Babalawo*, a high-ranking male priest. He throws an *ekwele* on the ground and gets meaning from how the 8 pieces of this chain fall and hit the floor. The priests of this religion are also extremely knowledgeable about herbs and traditional medicine, and they play a key role in the community when it comes to health.

Vodou and Candomble

In Vodou, you have the Lwa. In Candomble, you have the *Orixa,* who are African deities. This spelling is based on the Portuguese phonetic spelling of the Yoruba *Orisa* (pronounced oh-ree-sha.) Many Orixa venerated in Brazil are the same as the ones you find in Benin and western Nigeria, Yoruba land.

In Vodou, you have Bondye as the supreme creator God. In Candomble, above the Orixa is the creator God, Olorun. After the Orixa, you have Oxala, who has a special role in the creation of man. Oxala shows up as an aggressive young man and a peaceful old man. He is compared to Jesus, Friday, and the color white.

Axe or Ache is the spiritual energy found in all parts of nature, apparitions, and gods and humans can take it up. It is existence's mystical power, found in the material and the symbolic, plants and animals, and even inorganic matter. There are rituals you can do to boost the Orixa and Axe and then transfer them to humans. When concentrated, Axe is found in animal blood and intestines, and that's why believers and ritual objects are baptized with animal blood during Candomble festivities. At the end of the ceremony, everyone gets to enjoy a meal made from sacrificed animals. This meal is very important, as it is full of Axe.

Is Voodoo Hoodoo?

Vodou is a religion, but Hoodoo is just southern folk magic that uses the magical methods of the Congolese of Africa with none of the religion. There's no such thing as the Lwas, orishas, or nkisi. Interestingly, those who practice Hoodoo are often Protestant Christians. They're also known as conjurers or root workers. They make jack balls or mojo bags, both of which are magical charms. They work with herbal cleansing baths, magical powders, lamps, and candles to do their spells. They do all this while praying to God the Father and Jesus while singing Psalms. While many Hoodoo practitioners are Protestant Christians, some Catholic practitioners will make their petitions to Catholic saints. This doesn't make them Vodouisants, as they're petitioning the actual saints who aren't syncretized for any African spirit or deity. Long story short: Hoodoo isn't Vodou.

Racism and Stereotyping of African Traditional Religions

It's rather unfortunate that colonial stereotypes and racism have victimized African Traditional Religions for hundreds of years. This is no accident. The dehumanization of Africans is a deliberate attempt to make African religions seem demonic and barbaric. This way, the rest of the world would come to think of Africans as being less than human. It would then be easier on everyone's conscience to continue uprooting Africans from their loves and lives to use them as slaves.

The racist depictions of Haitian Vodou and other African traditional religious practices make the religions seem demonic. The culprits portray these beliefs and practices as no more than a bunch of dark magicians turning people into zombies. They make it seem that Vodou is all about hurting people with Vodou dolls, making pacts with Satan, and eating the flesh of other humans. The interesting thing about dolls in magic is that they were originally used in European witchcraft. None of these African religions acknowledge the existence of Satan or any other devil, neither do they worship Satan. These depictions in movies are racist, meant to incite fear and disdain in the hearts and minds of Europeans and even Africans who are unaware of their roots.

The very idea of "black magic" is racist. It is rooted in labeling Africans as black and tagging every religious practice from Africa as evil. So how do you refer to magic which is meant to cause harm? Just call it harmful magic or bad magic.

The only reason that impression exists today is that the slavers worked long and hard to paint these traditions in a negative light. We must ask ourselves about how one religious system is superior to anyone else's. What makes Catholicism or Christianity any more valid than Haitian Vodou?

Chapter 9: Vodou Festivals and Celebrations

Bmcao2, CC BY-SA 4.0 https://creativecommons.org/licenses/by-sa/4.0 via Wikimedia Commons
https://commons.wikimedia.org/wiki/File:Haitian_Carnival_(Kanaval).jpg

There's no better way to understand a culture and what makes it different from the rest than to explore its holidays and how they are celebrated. Have you ever thought about what the Haitian holidays are like? Or which ones might have some similarity with the European and American holidays? What about the festivals that are so unique you couldn't possibly experience them anywhere but Haiti? Vodou ceremonies can be very exciting and colorful. All the fun aside, they're meant to help the Vodouisants find their way to the light of divinity. In this chapter, we'll go over some of these celebrations.

List of Vodou Celebrations

January 2, 3, and 4: Case gateaux (breaking the cakes). This is a communicable version of Mange Loa.

January 6: Les Rois (also called the kings).

February 25: Manger tetes d'l'eau.

March 16: Loko Davi.

March 19: Saint Joseph's day.

March 20: Legba Zaou (devotees mostly eat a black goat on this day).

April 27: Damballah Wedo.

April 29: Casse Canarie (breaking the jugs). This is to mark the deliverance of all souls in purgatory.

April 31: Mange les morts (feeding the dead)

May 12: Mange Loa (feeding of different Loa)

May 18: Feeding Grande Aloumandia

May 20 and 21: Simbi blanc

May 30: Chante masses

June 24: Saint John's day

June 28: Mystere Grande Delai; Monsieur Guimeh Sauveur. A table is served for Maetresse Mam'bo, Mattress Tenaise; and Maetresse Erzulie

July 25: Papa Ogou (goats and sheep are given as offerings)

July 26: Grande Aloumandia; Mystere Grande Delai

July 29: Maetresse Lorvana; Maetresse Silverine

August 25: A communion table is served for Damballah wedo

August 29: L'Orient

August 30 and 31: Agwe (he is offered peppermints, peppers, and goats)

September 25: Mousondi and Roi Wangol

September 29: Manman Aloumadia

September 30: Mattresse Delai

November 1 and 2: Fet Guede. On this day, the Guede Loa emerge from the cemeteries, take over their horses, and amuse themselves as souls reincarnated or incarnated

November 25: Manger yam

December 10: Ganga-Bois

December 12, 13, and 14: Agoueh r oyo (feeding the sea)

December 25: Bath of Christmas.

Now let's take a look at some of these festivals in detail

New Years' Day: This is one of the biggest parties thrown by Haitians. The celebrations take place over an entire week, with devotees decorating their homes with lights and flowers.

Every holiday, families gather around a well-set table of food like cherries, pineapple slices, holiday ham, *diri ak djon djon* (also called black rice), stewed turkey, fried plantain, cassava, soup joumou, and yucca. Once they pass around a bottle of alcohol like Rhum Barbancourt, they get into interesting conversations about life in Haiti and all of the things connected to the state of Haiti.

This festival is so much more than just marking a new year, though. It was the day that Haiti finally freed itself from the French and became the very first black nation to gain independence. In celebration of this event, Marie-Claire Heureuse Felicite made a proclamation: On this day, not one Haitian is to go without having a bowl of soup joumou (pumpkin soup). This delicious and colorful meal is always on the menu during the celebration. She was the wife of Jean-Jacque Dessalines, who was one of the revolution's leaders.

Most Holidays in Haiti are loosely defined, some of them are on calendars (or not) one year, and the next year it's different. These holidays are basically either a Vodou celebration, or a Christian celebration, or more often, both.

Plaine du Nord: This is a festival that takes place year after year in July. The Kreyol speakers know this celebration as the Plen Dino Festival. Plen du Nord is also the name of a settlement between the Atlantic Ocean and the Massif de Nord mountain on the country's northern border. The little town is mostly a Maroon and Creole community that has done an excellent job of preserving African traditions.

The festival isn't named after this little town just because that's where it happens. It's also where the revolution that led to the independence of Haiti and the freedom of slaves began. Everyone, slave and free, reached out to the Lwa they worshipped for their blessing and favor to start the war that would lead to everyone being free.

This festival is also a celebration of Ogou, the Yoruba and Benin warrior god of iron. Over two days, all devotees make their way to a sacred mud pool called Saint Jacques Hole. Here, a number of them will take spiritual and magical baths and experience a spiritual rebirth. They show up with offerings for the gods, while the mambos and houngans show up with bullocks meant to be sacrificed. Sheep, cows, goats, and chickens are also offered to the gods.

Some devotees prefer to wear red, black, or other dark colors. In contrast, the mambo and houngan wear colors that align with the purpose of their rituals for that event. Those who want a spiritual bath are helped by the mambo or houngan, who bathes them in the mud pool and prays with them as well. They use incense for these rituals.

Children also show up at these rituals and are held upside down while being bathed.

Once the bath is over, the Vodouisants make offerings to the Lwa, close to the mud hole's cross. The mambo will be the first to kill her bullock, then other junior houngans and mambos can sacrifice the animals their congregation brought along. The blood is used to appease the gods, make them happy, wash all sin, and act as an investment of sorts into a year with good health, prosperity, and other wonderful things. The blood is poured on whoever brought the offering, and then they pray and give thanks for a successful festival.

By nightfall, there's dancing and singing by candlelight which signifies the presence of the ancestors and gods during the whole ceremony. During this time, some devotees enter a trance state and begin saying and doing things they do not recall afterward. There's not much drinking and eating during this festival for a good reason. The fast is meant as an homage to the warriors who won them their freedom.

The festival allows people to feel what it was like for those who fought the slavers and their accomplices. As it's closely linked to several Vodou celebrations in West Africa and has suffered from smear campaigns, the festival is deemed evil and dark, but that is not the case.

Ouidah Voodoo Festival: This festival takes place in Ouidah, Benin. The main activities happen close to the "Point of No Return" monument on the beach on January 10. Thousands of devotees head to this location to be blessed by the chief priest. They slaughter a goat in honor of the spirits, sing, chant, dance, and beat drums. Their costumes are quite a visual treat, but the gin is rather rough.

Benin is known as the home of West African Vodou, so when you're around the country on January 10, it's worth checking out this festival (also called the Fete du Vodoun). It is one of the festivals that draws many tourists. The Fon people are the ones who organize the festival. The Voodoo Festival is a recognized public holiday that the entire country celebrates. Still, there's no procession as popular as the ones in Ouidah. It starts with a goat being slaughtered – and then comes the rest of it.

The festival is meant to honor the lives stolen by the slave trade. The *feticheur* or chief priest at this festival starts off the main event only after giving honor, where it's due, at the Temple of Pythons. The procession follows the same route that slaves were transported west from Benin, ending at Ouidah beach, overlooking the Atlantic. There, many Vodou groups pay their respects to Dagbo and the other powerful chief priests present. You can see the traditional masks, ceremonial drums, jewelry, and colorful outfits as part of this festival. You will also find zangbetos, watchmen of the night who wear outfits much like haystacks, animal sacrifices, and devotees dressed resembling the Lwa.

Voodoofest: This is at Voodoo Authentica, which is a French Quarter shop in New Orleans. It takes place on October 21. You will find educational and cultural presentations, workshops on doll making and drumming, and meetings with the leading voodooists in the city. An ancestral healing ritual wraps up the day.

Carnival: It is one of the biggest celebrations in Haiti, named after the Latin word *carnavale,* which means "meat farewell." It's also called Defile Kanaval. For several weeks, Port-au-Prince and other cities in Haiti become radically different. The same happens across the world where other carnivals are happening.

The celebrations begin at January's end and end with Mardi Gras or "Fat Tuesday." This is when across all homes in Haiti, different kinds of fat are eaten. After Fat Tuesday, it is Ash Wednesday, a Catholic holiday that is the beginning of lent; during Carnival, you'll experience fun music, parades full of color, and traditional dances and art throughout Haiti.

Kanaval is basically the start of one of the holiest periods of the year. At this time, everyone repents for their wrongdoing and becomes very prayerful, seeking forgiveness. The idea of this festival is to have fun, forget about the worries and troubles life brings you, and express yourself in dance and song. Some popular Kanaval phrases you now know are *sote,* meaning "jump up," and *mete men nan le,* meaning "put your hands in the air." At this time, popular musicians like Wyclef Jean and Rihanna return home to perform their music.

Leve nom: This is also called "taking the name." It's when magical protection and talismans are given to the young, who then take on an ancestor's name to keep the tradition alive. The spirit that's been entrusted with the child's safety is to remain with them for life.

Metta n'anme: Also known as "placing the soul," this ritual involves balancing a newborn's ba and ka, which are the two parts of one's soul.

Lave-tete: This ritual is called "washing the head." It is essentially a baptism that makes it possible for the Lwa to "enter the head" of those who are newly initiated to the way. Water happens to be the Lwa's pathway to humans.

Garde: This is a magical affirmation of the Leve nom — being the Lwa that protects the souls entrusted to it and to whom the people must make sacrifices as a way of appreciating their protection.

Mange Lwa: Every ceremony where animals are offered qualifies as a Mange Lwa, which translates to "the feeding of the Lwa." That being said, Mange Lwa is generally a large, yearly event at which all the Lwa are offered syrups, drinks, chickens, birds, bulls, and other things. The celebration takes place from January 2 to 3. It's also called "case gateaux" or "the breaking of the cakes." Vodouisants firmly believe the Lwa's powers become even stronger on Earth when these celebrations occur.

Fete Gede: This celebration is also called All Souls' Day. It's one of Haiti's national holidays, marked on November 1 and 2. Vodouisants head to the main cemetery in the city to make their offerings of flowers, candles, food, and drink; pray to the ancestors; and light candles for the ones who have passed on. The rest of the dancing and celebration goes on at the peristil all through the night. They also thank the Gede and ancestors for all the good they've experienced throughout the past year. The festival involves lots of wild dancing reminiscent of sexual intercourse, so you want to keep that in mind.

The devotees make altars dedicated to the dead, both public and private, in various homes. The usual practice is in the morning on November 1, when people head off to church. When they get home, they dress up like the Guedes. This means their outfits are either ragtag or very elegant like Baron Samedi. They also paint their faces and then head out to town. Other than just worship at the cemetery, they make a point of cleaning their ancestors' tombs thoroughly.

You can draw many parallels between this festival and the Mexican Dia de Muertos or Day of the Dead. For instance, Fete Gede is the result of a blending of Haitian Vodou and Catholic practices. The Mexican Day of the Dead is a blend of pre-Hispanic culture and Catholicism. Altars are necessary for both celebrations, as are alcohol, food, certain colors, and pictures. Another thing they have in common is the kind of items placed on the altars and the relevance of colors, even though colors may have different meanings in both practices. The colors used in Haiti are white, black, and purple, while orange is the predominant color in Mexico. These practices involve caring for loved ones' graves. The devotees create an atmosphere of happiness among the families who celebrate together. These similarities show that while certain aspects may be different in each celebration, it is very important to honor the ancestors.

Bath of Christmas: This particular Haitian Voodoo holiday is syncretized with Christmas, so December 25 is the day it's celebrated. Vodouisants wear talismans and rub medical treatment on themselves to bring them protection and good luck. Then it's time to sacrifice turkeys, goats, and pigs to the Lwa.

Grand Bois: This holiday is marked in honor of the great wood, Gran Bois; this is one of nature's elemental powers, connected to medicinal herbs and plants, as well as trees. Gran Bois is Vodou's answer to Saint Sebastian, whom the Catholic Church venerates as a protector from sickness and disease. On this day, the Vodouisants will offer Grand Bois spiced rum, honey, and herbs.

Festival of Yemanja: Yemanja or Yemoya is worshipped in Candomble, but she has a lot in common with Vodou. She is honored as the protector of sailors, fishermen, and children. About a million people dress in white at this festival and walk in a procession to the sea from Salvador's Rio Vermelho district. With them, they carry baskets of gifts for this Lwa. When they get to the water, they set their baskets in the sea and allow them to be carried away. The procession turns into a street party that goes on even into the night.

Rara: Just as in Europe or America, holidays may change dates. A good example of a holiday like this is Rara, which is Easter week. Rara is a word from an old American Indian celebration called *Bakororo*, which was full of chaos. As you know, "chaos" is hardly a word that would cross the average European or American's mind when you're talking about holy weeks. The celebration has many activities, from call and response singing to performances satirizing politics and fanciful, elaborate parades to display the Haitian way of celebrating Easter. Then there's also lovely food like rice, beans, yams, and fish.

The parade moves through the village with flutes, rattles, drums, and brass instruments. People wear wonderful and brand-new glittery costumes with knotted scarves. Every group in the parade is led by a *Kolomel* who picks the route. He issues commands with his whistle and cracks a whip when he senses the path needs to be purified from evil spirits hanging around. Each group also has an officer known as the *Majo Jonk*. This person has great dancing skills and a baton they twirl as they move.

Flag Day: Flags are usually common in parades. They symbolize the pride of their country, carried above their heads with the utmost respect. So, it's not surprising that this day is a very important one in Haiti. The very first Haitian flag is believed to have been created rather dramatically by Dessalines. He took the French flag's red, white, and blue, ripped out the white part, tossed it away, and told Catherine Flon, his god-daughter, to put the red and blue parts together. The blue represents the black people of Haiti, and the red is for the people of color. There's a holiday just like this one in honor of Jean-Jacques Dessalines death, on October 17.

Flag Day is a day full of veneration for Grandmother Aloumandia, also referred to as Great Saint Anne or Saint Soleil Haiti. The Haitians show their honor and respect for their ancestors by feeding her lovely traditional meals, celebrating with both family and the community.

Battle of Vertieres: Dessaline is the one general from the Haitian revolution, venerated in Haitian Vodou. There's another holiday on November 18, called the Batay Vetye or Battle of Vertieres. The battle was the last point where the great Dessalines defeated the French Army on November 18, 1803. This happened in a place which is now known as Cap-Haitien.

Christmas: You've probably already guessed that Haitian Christmas is different in some ways. At the start of December, Haitians will buy pine trees that have been freshly cut to use as Christmas trees. They'll decorate these trees with bright, beautiful ornaments and even set up an impressive nativity scene at the bottom of the tree. They also add colored lights, fix their homes, buy new stuff, and let their children play with new toys given to them by *Tonton Nwel*, who is basically Santa Claus.

The Haitian kids do it differently from American ones, who put out cookies and milk for Santa and hang up stockings by the fireplace. The Haitian kids will instead set their nice and clean shoes beneath the tree or on the porch. They fill these shoes with straw and leave them out, hoping that Santa will take out the straw and put presents in and around the shoes.

Interestingly, kids of all ages can drink anisette on Christmas Eve – a rum made from anise leaves and sugar. They also get to stay out of their homes late. In fact, most people will stay awake until 3 AM, as the entire neighborhood heads out caroling. The dinner held after Christmas Eve mass is called *reveillon* and will usually last till dawn.

Chapter 10: Vodou as a Way of Life

Vodou is much more than just a religion. It's a way of life that calls for service every single day. It's a tradition that's about action, something not just done but lived. You can't become a passive participant of Vodou. You have to immerse yourself completely in it.

The ceremonies are rooted in drumming, singing, dancing, salutes, tracing of veves, and sacrifices. It's not a tradition where you sit in a pew listening to someone preaching to you. Also, every day is sacred in Vodou, dedicated to a certain Lwa or a group of Lwa. Sunday belongs to Bondye, and what Vodouisants do on this day varies. Some might not bother saluting the Lwa and will not take part in any spiritual work. Others might make no bones about it being a sacred day, as they have other things to do. Still, even then, they continue to remember and honor God in all their activities.

There are many ways you could serve the Lwa on their days. You could wear their colors, decide to abstain from food or something else, sing in their honor, or perform some service to them. Vodouisants who are married to a Lwa have to keep that Lwa's day sacred. This might mean they have to dress a certain way, make their bed and food a certain way, or do other things to indicate their full commitment to their spirit spouse.

Monday is the beginning of the week for many, though it's the second day of the week. It's a day that is sacred to Legba, Gede, and the Ancestors. After you serve God on Sunday, it's time to serve your ancestors on Monday, and then you'll find all your workflows better for you — including spiritual work with your Lwa. This is where service to the Gede and the ancestors enters the picture. Before you can serve any of the Lwa, you must pay your respects to Legba, the gatekeeper, the one who opens and shuts your doors as he chooses.

Many Vodouisants take part in daily devotionals, especially if their main source of income is in service of the Lwa. You have to "wake them up" through service to get them to work on your behalf. This way, they bless you by opening up your home to attract clientele. There are many ways you could wake up your Lwa.

On Mondays, you should take all bowls and glasses of water off all your altars and toss them out your front door. Throw out the coffee you made for the Gede as well. Then wash the bowls, glasses, and the Gede's coffee cup, make some fresh coffee, and fill the bowls or other vessels with fresh, clean water. Then you light a candle and say your prayers. When you're done, you can converse with your Lwa, offer them water and coffee, and if you can, a libation of schnapps or rum.

Tuesdays are sacred to the Lwa Petwo, especially Ezili Danto. Wednesday is for Ogou and the Nago Nation; Thursday belongs to the Lwa Rada; Friday is also for the Gede, especially Brijit and Baron. Saturday is for every Lwa. You can create your own calendar for your devotion to the Lwa. You don't need more than five minutes for each day, but if you want to go longer, that's fine too. The more you work with the Lwa each day, the better your life will be.

There are many things you can and should do to truly live this tradition. One thing is certain about becoming a Vodouisant yourself: The way you think about the world will radically change. The more you practice, the more you'll learn to act in alignment with your true self. When faced with opposition, you'll know how to take care of the problem rather than brush it off. You face it with bravery and fix it because you know that you have the Lwa backing you up. Vodou is absolutely empowering.

Can Anyone Practice Vodou?

There's a saying among Vodouisants that goes, "Vodou is for everyone, but not everyone is for Vodou." Anyone can enjoy the healing and insight provided by the Lwa. Anyone can partake in a ceremony, dance, eat, and meet the Lwa. Everyone's invited, but not everyone can lead the festival, hold an asson, service the Lwa by allowing themselves to be possessed, and so on. In other words, while everyone is welcome, it isn't everyone who will truly be at home with the practice enough to completely embrace every aspect. In light of this fact, how can you become a part of this way of life? How do you know that you'll be here for the long haul, and not just a day or two? How can you be absolutely certain the Lwa calls you to serve them?

First Steps

It can be very difficult making the first move as you don't know what's right or wrong, what you should do, and where you should get help to learn the ways of Vodou. So, let's get into everything you need to know as you start your journey.

Before you start down this path, it helps to have some idea of where you're headed. First, you need to know if Vodou is what you seek. Most of the time, when people say they want to get into Vodou, they don't really mean they would like to explore this Haitian path. What they want is guidance on folk magic. Unfortunately, the magical practices of Blacks in the American South have been mislabeled. This causes many to assume the religion of Vodou is the same as hoodoo, which is "root work" or "conjure," a folk magic tradition.

You need to understand that Vodou is a religion with a priesthood and hierarchy. All magical and spiritual work is performed exclusively by the priesthood with the Lwa's assistance, and it's not something just everyone and anyone can do. However, when it comes to root work/conjure/hoodoo tradition, it's open to everyone who wants to learn because it's folk magic. So, if you want a folk magic system and you'd like to change your life by doing your own spiritual work, you should know that Vodou isn't for you. If you want to have a relationship with the Lwa, a family with connections to the spirits, a sense of community, and a life made more fulfilling through a great religion, then welcome.

Are the Lwa Calling You? How Should You Respond?

As Vodou is for everyone, it's not something that is only for Haitians. The Lwa can call anyone all over the world, no matter where you are. This means they can call even those who have no clue what Haitian culture is. It doesn't matter if you have no idea what it means to practice Vodou and have no information on the spirits summoning you to service. When they call you, it's because they want you.

Usually, those called by the Lwa will have dreams about them and feel driven to learn all they can about these spirits. The Gede or Legba usually play a huge part in drawing outsiders to Vodou. Legba is the one who must open up the gates to the Lwa, and the Guede is the universal spirit. It's not easy to find quality information on these being; Many use incorrect information on the internet to serve the Lwa on their own, but that's not the way to go.

If you really want to make progress with your Vodou path, you should seek the assistance of a houngan or mambo. They're the ones tasked with the job of interpreting the messages the Lwa has for you, and it's best to let them do it since you're as yet inexperienced and uninitiated. They're the ones who help connect humans with the divine, and it's their job to tell you the right information that will help you on your way. How do you know you're getting the right knowledge? Because they speak directly with the Lwa themselves. So, let a mambo or houngan do a proper reading for you.

The reading you need to do is known as an escort consultation. It's meant to help you learn the spirits walking with you, find out if they have something to tell you and what their message is. It's how you find out if you're called to Vodou, if you have to be initiated, and what exactly you're called to do. This means becoming either part of the priesthood or a hounsi. The hounsi are initiates and house members who serve the Lwa, help the mambo and houngan, and are possessed during ceremonies. You'll also learn the specific ways the Lwa would like to be served by you.

After the reading, the priest will guide you on what to do based on what the Lwa have shared. If you have to start working on a relationship with a certain Lwa, they'll tell you more about that spirit and what you should do to start your service to them. They'll also tell you what to do and what to expect if you have to be initiated. If you're supposed to be initiated, that means you'll need to find a suitable house and join it.

Finding a Mambo or Houngan to Do a Reading

There are big names that draw people, and there are frauds as well. Some people go to the closest priestess or priest they can find, with no concern for whether or not they're the right fit. Thankfully, we have the internet now, which means the world is smaller and more interconnected than ever before. This makes it easy for you to reach out to a reputable and genuine mambo or houngan. However, it makes it just as easy to fall into the hands of scammers, especially if you go for the Google ads or page 1 results. So, how do you make sure you're with the right sosyete or priest? How can you be sure they're for real?

You need to reach out for help from someone you trust completely. You need help from someone with spirits that sync with yours and guidance that you can't get from anyone else. This person needs to see more than you can and have a much longer reach than you do. If you feel like you have no one like this, don't despair. You actually do. His name is Legba. You can ask him to open the way to the right road that will lead you where you should be.

To ask for Legba's help, you need to have a connection or relationship with your ancestors, at least. They know you better than anyone else, and they want nothing but good for you. They're close, desire your success, and want you on the best path for yourself in life. They can influence the physical world and set you on the path to the right priest, so it doesn't hurt to connect with them. To build a relationship with them, honor them in everything you do. If you have access to their graves, make sure to clean them and offer them their favorite things, in general. You can also pour libations on the ground for them. If you want, you can light candles for them and just sit in silent fellowship.

To build a relationship with Legba, you can set up an altar for him. Make sure it's only for him, and keep his altar far from every other spirit's. It's a good idea to set the altar at the entrance of your home. Learn his songs, sing to him, speak with him, and offer him his favorite things: Sweet potatoes, smoked chicken, white yams, fresh fruit, strong black coffee with no sugar, and another cup of strong coffee with lots of sugar. He also enjoys pipes with tobacco and Cuban cigars. When you've built a relationship with him, you can then ask him to assist your ancestors with finding you the right priest. Or you can ask him to lead the way himself so you can find the people who will help you with your quest.

If the Gede calls you, then your ancestors will be of more help to you as the Gede are the spirits of those who have left this world. They might even take over your search themselves. To be clear, this doesn't mean you'll hear voices telling you where to go or that someone will come and find you out of the blue. You need to be active in your search and keep your eyes open to spot opportunities. You could join forums and groups online and find your answer there. You might notice you keep seeing a certain book over and over and then finally decide to read it and find what you seek. You may have a ream that shows you the way to go or be led by a series of events. Just keep your eyes and heart open, and pay attention.

After Your Reading

When the reading is done, you will have an idea of what to do next. You might need some money to go through the initiation rites and need to have spiritual work done on your behalf. Either way, here's what you need to do next: Build a better relationship with your Lwa under the guidance of the mambo. You can also go to a fet held in honor of a Lwa. At the fet, the sosyete comes together in celebration. There's dancing, praying, and calling on the Lwa to participate in the festivities. The Lwa then shows up by giving guidance, healing, and advice to those in attendance who need it. Some people don't even need a reading because the Lwa told them at a fet that they had to become initiates. However, it's still a good idea to have someone escort you and talk about it with a houngan.

The fet will allow you to see what Vodou is like when all kinds of people in a sosyete come together to make magic happen. You'll see how every member fits in to form a beautiful whole and how their skills and talents are used in service to Lwa and to Bondye's glory. If it calls your spirit, then you just may have found a home.

There is a chance that your journey will take you down a different, unexpected path, or you will find yourself with a different African traditional religion, or Vodou may be your final home, with prayer and the peristil. The extent to which the path opens up for you is up to Bondye and the Lwa, but how far you follow it is entirely your decision. If you do decide to go as far as it goes, you will never be alone for sure. You'll have an entire spiritual family and the Lwa showing you the way. You'll become a part of something big and beautiful, thanks to Vodou.

Finding the Right Vodou House for You

When you've attended a Vodou ceremony, you'll find that you have a better grasp of Haitian Vodou than ever before. You probably will be brimming with questions, drawn to more ceremonies, checking out various sosyetes or houses. You might find Vodou interesting somewhere along the way, but it isn't for you because you're only interested in attending a fet now and then. Or you may decide Vodou is what you've been looking for all your life and that you're ready to join a sosyete or house.

Finding a house that is okay with letting you observe their practices can be a long, sometimes arduous process. In the same way, finding a house that will accept you as a family member can be difficult. Vodou isn't a school you get to be a student of only to graduate and do other things. You should know it might take a while to find a house. You might have to travel, try many options, and then some. Some people head all the way to Haiti to learn where the Lwa want you to stay.

However, you shouldn't let all of the time and effort dissuade you. It could happen quickly, or it could take time, but either way, if you're truly meant to serve the Lwa, know that they will make it happen for you. As Vodouisants say, "Si se Bondye ki voye oi, li peye fre ou." In English: "If it's God that sends you, He'll pay your expenses." All you need to do is keep your eyes, ears, and heart open.

The thing you need to know is that there's no such thing as "the right Vodou house." There's only one that's right for you. We're all different, and for this reason, we can't all belong to the same sosyete or family. There's no such thing as the one true lineage or family or initiation, no matter what any fake houngan or mambo would like to tell you. Each house is valid in its own right. You have to go out there and find one that is a good fit for you, and as there are many houses, this is a process that will take some time. All you have to do is to be patient. While you're still searching, you can still attend ceremonies and festivals as a show of service to the Lwa in your own little way.

Vodou houses have the regleman in common. So, if you find a house that flaunts this or espouses practices that no other house partakes in, then you might want to hold your horses on joining them. Chances are you'll find other reasons not to join that one. If you feel doubt or fear, then you should continue searching.

Being an outsider means you might be considered someone to be taken advantage of by shady people. Haitian Vodou has its own frauds, bigots, and con artists plaguing it. This is typical of every spiritual tradition. Understand this, ask your questions politely, and if something seems unclear, don't be afraid to ask again. Check what you learn from one Vodouisant or house against what others have to say, and you'll be less likely to get swindled or misled. As you ask, please refrain from discussing how some other mambo, houngan, or house does their own thing. If you do, you might get the hard sell where they try to convince you to stay because they don't practice that way. You might also come across as an opportunist or gossip, mouthing off about how houses aren't doing it right.

There's no way to sugarcoat this: Some houngans and mambos are inherently mistrustful of those who aren't natives. It doesn't matter how sincere you may come across. Some flat-out refuse non-Haitians. Some will try to make you partake in a sham initiation known derisively as "an American asson." Others will allow non-Haitians to be part of their sosyete but never initiate them. In this case, all they want is your money, and all you're getting is a lighter wallet. So, always keep your eyes open and ask questions, and you'll be less likely to be defrauded or led down the wrong path. Say a simple prayer to your spirits to guide you on your search, and trust what they tell you through your gut feelings.

Questions to Ask Before Joining a House

The following are questions that the houngan or mambo should be glad to answer, giving you details without feeling insulted or suspicious. Just remember to be polite and sincere.

How long have you been a practicing Vodouisant? You want to weigh every other answer they give you by the one you get here. The more experience they have, the more knowledgeable they should be.

At what point along your journey did you become a houngan or a mambo, and who initiated you? Every priesthood member is always proud of their lineage. This means they should have no problem answering these questions and telling you the ranks they've taken or received. You can ask to speak with their initiator so that their spiritual parents can verify them for you. You may need to speak Kreyol and make international calls if the initiator is part of older clergy. You might find it important to know whether the priest was initiated in Haiti or somewhere else. Most lineages insist that some or all initiation rituals take place on the island, while others accept initiations outside Haiti.

How many members are there in your house?

How many Vodouisants have you personally initiated, and may I speak with them? If you want to speak with the initiated kids or siblings, the house leader would be happy to give you information to reach them. Sometimes, especially when red flags pop up as you interview them, you might want to speak with the former members of the house too. Keep in mind that being with a house for many years doesn't necessarily mean that it's a great house to be in. However, the odds are low that a new priest with little experience as an initiate would have all the knowledge needed to run the house successfully on their own. They may work with their initiatory parents for a while as an apprentice before going off on their own.

On the flip side, they might simply continue to work with their spiritual parents permanently. If a houngan or mambo has no initiatory kids or house and claims to work on their own, then you should be suspicious and ask more questions. Another red flag is a house with fewer current members than former ones or too many initiates who don't stick around for long.

What are the services and ceremonies performed or offered by your house? Can I attend? Where can I find your peristil? Some houses have all the services of Haitian Vodou. In contrast, others are satellites of larger houses with their headquarters someplace else. This is why you need to know where the ceremonies happen, how far away they are, and how often they hold. If your house's headquarters is outside Haiti, you need to know if they do services in Haiti and if you can take part in it. You also need to know the requirements for attending ceremonies and if there are mandatory ones.

What do you expect of those who want to be part of your sosyete? Asking this question makes the priest realize that you understand being a part of their family is a two-way thing and that what you have to offer the house is as important as what it can offer you. Pay close attention to their philosophy on this, and notice what they emphasize. Notice if all they talk about is how what you can have for a fee or your time. Does it feel like everyone is treated with respect, whether or not they are Haitian? Does it feel like the family members cooperate with one another? Does the priest ask you questions, and do the questions make you feel more or less at ease?

Which Lwa is your lineage or house devoted to? This may or may not help you with choosing the house. The regleman makes it clear that all lineages and houses serve every Lwa of Ginen. Still, the houses have patron Lwa. Some have Lwa that make an appearance so often that they're deemed the papa or mama spirits of the family. The characters of the spirits affect the whole sosyete. This is the case even if some of the members don't serve that Lwa too often. When Petro spirits rule a house, it might not be a good fit for someone who leans towards the Rada.

Conclusion

We've come to the end of this book at last, but this could be the start of something special for you. Do consider getting a reading, and if you're led to do so, seek out a house. Before we wrap this up, you should press with more questions when you notice a red flag – and be very open and ready to look elsewhere. You also need to trust your gut and notice how you feel about a house. Consider the interviews you do with the present and former members and elders as well. What's your assessment of the house? Is it a hit or miss? Here are red flags to watch out for:

Too much emphasis on money. Beware of this, especially when it feels like you're getting less for more money. Are you being asked to pay more for things you've already paid for? Have you noticed that initiation to this house is based on whether or not you have cash available? Or has it been suggested to you that you can have whatever rank you want for the right price? Are you constantly being asked for cash? If you notice simple, small divinations that quickly morph into dire proclamations, be careful. You're being scammed if every other day, you're told something like, "You're in a world of trouble now, and only the Lwa can save you. They want you to do this, that, and the other, and it will cost you more money." Suppose the house tells you that you've been cursed, and you have no choice but to be initiated or pay an arm and a leg for a special ritual or spiritual protection. In that case, you should definitely get a second, third, and even a fourth opinion before you fork over any cash.

The constant insistence that a house or lineage is the one and only true place for Vodou. An open house wouldn't claim they're better than others or try to put down other houses by saying they don't do Vodou right. They can take pride in their home, of course. There's nothing wrong with that. However, if they insist there's no place as good as theirs, then you should probably leave. No true priestess or priest make other lineages and houses look bad. They're busy dedicating their time and attention to serving the Lwa and helping their kids and clients as they should.

An air of instability, misery, and dissatisfaction in the house. Life in Haiti is hard, but serving the Lwa brings happiness and comfort, as the Lwa care for their own. Be wary of a house that's always moving from one trouble to another. If the house is full of crisis or unhappy and angry people with too much drama, then that means something's off. It's a sign that there's something they're not doing right or are neglecting.

Excess complaining and slander of former members. When a house is stable and busy, there's really no time for anyone to whine about how horrible some mambo or hounsi is or used to be. Anything beyond simple and factual statements or direct answers to questions is a cause for concern. You don't want to be in a house that spends too much time badmouthing former members because that house isn't serving the Lwa. It's also a preview of things to come when you decide to leave the house. You don't want that sort of treatment, so you shouldn't condone it just because they're talking about someone else.

The same goes for current members. Some mambos and houngans speak ill of their own children, complaining about them. This is not the way it should be. There's no room for dysfunction in the sosyete. You want to be part of a house where you're sure your parents truly love you. Does this mean you should never have disagreements? Of course not; they're unavoidable. However, the way these disagreements are handled says a lot about the character of a family.

Beware of a house that significantly disregards the regleman in ways that are neither supported by common sense or Vodou practice. Often, expatriate Haitians or non-Haitians lead these houses. Still, the truth is both within and outside Haiti, sosyetes will follow the regleman as much as possible. For instance, a house may claim that their Lwa doesn't eat meat, but the truth is that they decided not to feed the Lwa meat. Some houses won't serve Petro because they think of them as devils, but as you already know, that's ridiculous. Then there are houses within and outside Haiti that are in the process of creating "new forms of Vodou." The Lwa may truly lead them to do things differently. However, you should know that those practices aren't fundamentally Haitian Vodou. So, if you notice the house doesn't get the difference between Haitian Vodou and other forms, beware. Even worse, if they try to tell you that Haitians aren't doing it right, then you should be concerned.

Say you've gotten all the information you need, asked all your questions, and joined the ceremonies. Keep in mind that what happens next is entirely up to you, and no one other than you can or should make decisions for you about what you do with your spiritual life. So, pay attention to what your heart says. You can get readings and reach out to the spirits yourself to help you. Keep a dream journal, and let the Lwa and ancestors communicate with you. If you're meant to be a Vodouisant, then you will be.

Here's another book by Mari Silva that you might like

Your Free Gift (only available for a limited time)

Thanks for getting this book! If you want to learn more about various spirituality topics, then join Mari Silva's community and get a free guided meditation MP3 for awakening your third eye. This guided meditation mp3 is designed to open and strengthen ones third eye so you can experience a higher state of consciousness. Simply visit the link below the image to get started.

https://spiritualityspot.com/meditation

References

Cosentino, Donald J. Sacred Arts of Haitian Vodou. Los Angeles: UCLA Fowler Museum of

Cultural History,

1995.

Deren, Maya. Divine Horsemen: The Living Gods of Haiti. London: Thames and Hudson, 1953.

Deren, Maya. Divine Horsemen: The Living Gods of Haiti. London: Thames and Hudson, 1953.

Filan, Kenaz. The Haitian Vodou Handbook: Protocols for Riding With the Lwa. Rochester, VT:

Destiny Books,

2007.

Filan, Kenaz. The Haitian Vodou Handbook: Protocols for Riding With the Lwa. Rochester, VT:

Destiny Books,

2007.

Olmos, Margarite Fernandez, and Lizabeth Paravasini-Gebert. Creole Religions of the

Caribbean: An Introduction

from Vodou and Santeria to Obeah and Espiritismo. New York: New York University Press,

2003.

Turlington, Shannon. The Complete Idiot's Guide to Voodoo. New York: Alpha Books, 2001.

Awolalu, J. Omosade. Yorùbá Beliefs & Sacrificial Rites. Brooklyn, NY: Athelia Henrietta

Press, 1996.

González-Wippler, Migene. Santería: the Religion. St. Paul, MN: Llewellyn, 1989.

Malbrough, Ray. Hoodoo Mysteries: Folk Magic, Mysticism and Rituals. St. Paul, MN:

Llewellyn, 2003.

Voeks, Robert A. Sacred Leaves of Candomble: African Magic, Medicine, and Religion in

Brazil. Austin, TX:

University of Texas Press, 1997

Printed in Great Britain
by Amazon

04c6a29e-116f-4b3c-befd-ca83cf88f4a4R01